9\19

4/-

S0-AHZ-401

The Perfect Child for Us

Linda Sprague Pappas

Gracednotes Ministries
405 Northridge Street NW
North Canton, Ohio 44720

© 2019 Linda Sprague Pappas

Cover Design: Jill Leonard McAmis

Scripture quotations, unless otherwise indicated, are taken from the
Holy Bible, New International Version®, NIV®.
Copyright ©1973, 1978, 1984, 2011 by Biblica, Inc.™
Used by permission of Zondervan.
All rights reserved worldwide. www.zondervan.com
The "NIV" and "New International Version" are trademarks regis-
tered in the United States Patent and Trademark Office by
Biblica, Inc.™

ALL RIGHTS RESERVED. This book contains material protected
under International and Federal Copyright Laws and Treaties. Any
unauthorized reprint or use of this material is prohibited. No part of
this book may be reproduced or transmitted in any form or by any
means, electronic or mechanical, including photocopying, record-
ing, or by any information storage and retrieval system without ex-
press written permission from the author / publisher.

Printed in the United States

ISBN:13- 978-1731285959

Dedicated with love to my family:

Jay

Lindsay, Rick, and Cate

Laurie, Zach, and Caden

Chapter 1

"For you created my inmost being; you knit me together in my mother's womb. I praise you because I am fearfully and wonderfully made."
Psalm 139:13-14

Looking down into a clear plastic bassinet, I got my first glimpse of Caden Zachary, our newborn grandson. On an early February morning before sunrise, my husband Jay and I stood in the corridor outside the newborn nursery at Rex Hospital in Raleigh, North Carolina, eagerly greeting the newest member of our family. For what seemed like a very long time, we had anxiously paced up and down the hallway awaiting his birth. Nearby our daughter lay in the operating room having a C-section.

Finally, when we thought we couldn't stand the suspense for another minute, a young nurse in blue scrubs appeared around the corner. She rapidly pushed Caden's bassinet towards us as our son-in-law Zach jogged nervously alongside. As she paused to give Jay and me, the proud grandparents, a good first look, I stared down into Caden's soulful eyes, wide open and alert. Wearing only a diaper, his body looked flawless. His creamy, rosy complexion even lacked the usual blotches and wrinkles of a newborn. With a quivering lip, he let out a few mournful cries. The sound he made was so weak and soft, barely a murmur in the early dawn quiet of the hospital hallway. No lusty squall. Instead he sounded exactly like a tiny mewling puppy. Zach, our son-in-law, smiled proudly. The friendly nurse standing by his elbow also grinned with the pleasure of introducing this new baby to his excited grandparents.

Although my first thoughts were that Caden looked absolutely perfect, a quiver of apprehension suddenly fluttered in my stomach. My mother's intuition whispered a warning: *Caden is lying so still.* His arms and legs stretched out motionless. His cry sounded strange. Something I couldn't put my finger on didn't seem quite right.

Jay and I had been looking forward to this little guy's arrival for months. He was our first grandson and the first child of our younger daughter Laurie and her husband Zach.

Laurie and Zach had met in college at Capital University in Bexley, Ohio, a suburb of Columbus. Both of them grew up in families with a Lutheran religious tradition, and they found Capital, a small Lutheran liberal arts school with a strong academic and athletic program, to be just the right place for them. Laurie was a sophomore and Zach a junior when they first caught each other's eye in the student union. From that moment on they were inseparable.

Both were involved in extracurricular campus activities. Zach, who ran cross country in high school in his hometown of Bowling Green, Ohio, continued to run for Capital. Laurie cheered him on at his meets but had trouble sharing his enthusiasm for running herself. Her love was dance. During her freshman year in college, she danced with a Capital dance team that performed at halftime shows during basketball season. In high school she had danced with a similar group, which she felt was even superior to Capital's team. Consequently, her sophomore year she went looking for a more challenging dance experience. She found what she wanted in another college organization called Orchesis, a dance company that had two big yearly performances, one in conjunction with the Capital University Jazz Band and another a spring recital. These performances were much more professional, and they also provided a better outlet for her personal creative style.

Laurie and Zach both liked being active, and they used their involvement in running and dancing to stay physically fit. Never satisfied with less than A's, Laurie tended to get very stressed with her college classes. Dancing provided a healthy outlet for her competitive drive and any excess emotional energy.

Zach graduated from Capital a year ahead of Laurie and entered The Ohio State University College of Dentistry in the fall of 2002. When Laurie graduated in May the following year, they got engaged with plans to marry in August of 2004. As the year after her graduation progressed, Laurie busied herself with wedding plans and starting her first real job in public relations at Lutheran Social Services in Columbus.

During that time Zach began to question his own career choice. Although he loved science and definitely had an aptitude for it – he had passed a rigorous, required academic exam for second-year dental students on the first try – he was beginning to wonder whether or not he really wanted to be a dentist. After much thought, he made the difficult decision the fall after they were married to leave dental school and pursue a different profession.

Jay and I were just as supportive as Laurie was. In fact, we encouraged him to follow his heart. Nevertheless, making a major career move wasn't easy. Zach was newly married, and he took that responsibility very seriously. To drop out of dental school halfway through required a huge leap of faith. The dean of the dental school suggested that he just take a leave of absence, but Zach knew in his heart that being a dentist was no longer his dream. He left the university and immediately began searching for a promising new career opportunity.

About six months later in the spring of 2005, Zach took a job as a DNA analyst and was eventually promoted to forensic biologist at the North Carolina State Crime Lab outside of Raleigh. He and Laurie rented a two-bedroom apartment in a large new complex in Garner, a suburb of Raleigh, and Laurie started working as a Special Events Coordinator for a nonprofit in Raleigh. They loved the area's warm weather, the outdoor activities, and the proximity to Wilmington and the Atlantic beaches that their new location provided.

Eventually Laurie began considering a career change of her own. They had been in Raleigh for several years, and she was working for another nonprofit. The job involved planning and producing six large special events over the course of the year as well as maintaining the web page and publishing a monthly magazine for the organization. In addition, she was in charge of all the volunteers for each event. Always a perfectionist, she found it hard to rely on others to do the tasks that she often felt she could do better herself. The job became very stressful and not particularly rewarding. Office politics were also taking their toll on her mental health, and finally she decided to resign. She wanted to find a new career that would be more personally fulfilling and meaningful.

In 2008, after much soul searching, Laurie decided to retrain as a medical massage therapist. She went back to school for nine months of hard work in the classroom. Science had never been her natural strong suit, but she studied hard and applied her excellent work ethic to this new goal. Her determination paid off, and she graduated with honors. After passing her state boards, she immediately was offered a job working in a chiropractor's office.

The previous spring she and Zach had bought their first house in Flowers Plantation, a family-friendly neighborhood outside of Clayton, North Carolina, on the outskirts of Raleigh. Their neighbors were other young families, who soon became their best friends. They joined a new and growing Methodist church filled with lots of members their own age. Before long they had adjusted easily to life in the suburbs. After six years of marriage, they finally felt settled. They had a house and two good jobs. The time seemed right to start their family.

Laurie got pregnant almost immediately. Except for the occasional aches and pains, mostly caused by performing a physically demanding job with an ever-expanding belly, her early pregnancy was relatively uneventful. Laurie, however, was not easily reassured that all was well and constantly fretted over every change in her body. Despite the normal blood tests, the textbook blood pressure readings, and the ultrasounds showing a perfectly-developing baby boy, Laurie worried relentlessly. She called me almost every day for reassurance, and I tried my best to provide it.

Her constant anxiety reminded me of when I had been a new mom myself to her older sister Lindsay. I became overly concerned every time Lindsay ran a fever because our own respected pediatrician, Dr. Murthi, had warned me to take fevers seriously.

"If the baby has a fever and her neck seems stiff, we assume meningitis until proven otherwise," he warned.

That admonition really scared me. How would I know if my infant had a stiff neck? Every fever, no matter how mild, sent me into a panic. During one office visit I confessed to him how afraid I was of my baby coming down with that awful disease.

He calmed my nervous mommy worries with this mantra, "Rare diseases rarely happen. That's why they are called rare."

Relating this story to Laurie, I soothed, "Quit worrying; everything will be just fine."

Later those glib reassurances haunted me.

The only real concern as she entered her final months of pregnancy was Caden's persistent breech position. He's just being stubborn like his momma, I thought. Eventually he'll flip around.

At first Laurie's obstetrician agreed and wasn't the least bit concerned either.

"Babies are often breech. He'll probably turn around on his own before delivery," he reassured her.

When that didn't happen, however, he and Laurie discussed the possibility of trying to manually turn Caden before she went into labor. After hearing the details of what that involved, Laurie decided turning Caden sounded miserable and uncomfortable for her and perhaps even too risky for Caden. Sometimes it could bring on early labor. Besides, the doctor couldn't even assure her that the procedure would work or that Caden wouldn't just flip back into a breech position again.

They decided to wait a little longer before making any decision, and we all kept hoping Caden would move into the proper position himself. Unfortunately, as her due date approached, baby Caden's head remained firmly planted under Laurie's left rib. As Laurie's pregnancy neared full term and after further discussion of the options with her doctor, a C-section was scheduled for the second week in February.

"Any particular day?" her OB wanted to know.

"Any day but Valentine's Day," Laurie said.

She herself had been born on New Year's Eve and knew the drawbacks of a holiday birthday. As if being born right after Christmas wasn't bad enough when it came to getting individual attention and actual birthday gifts, all the people she wanted to make a fuss over her birthday seemed to be out celebrating with others on New Year's Eve. The parents of her friends were more interested in going out for the evening themselves than taking their child to Laurie's birthday party. Even her aunt, uncle, cousins, and grandparents often had other plans on her special day. Nobody ever seemed available for her celebration, and no amount of consoling on my part ever made her happy with the day she'd been born.

So, with that request in mind, the doctor chose February 15 for Laurie's C-section. Caden, however, had other plans. Laurie went into labor the evening of February 13, just hours after Jay and I arrived in Clayton for the birth. We had all gone out to dinner at a favorite neighborhood Italian restaurant. No sooner were we back home than Laurie started to complain about her back hurting. It soon became apparent that this wasn't any ordinary backache. By 10:30 PM she and Zach were headed off to the hospital. Jay and I soon followed. At 3:00 AM on February 14, 2011, Caden made his appearance, a mere thirty-two hours before his scheduled delivery. No one complained about his Valentine's Day birth. We were all just thrilled that he had arrived.

Now I stood watching as Zach followed the nurse pushing Caden in a bassinet through the swinging doors into the newborn nursery. Jay and I moved towards the hall window where we could observe Caden's initial examination. Our daughter Laurie was still in the surgical area but was doing fine. She would be in recovery for a while longer and then taken to her room. The clock said 3:15 AM.

Quietly we observed the nurse measure, weigh, test, and check our little guy over from head to toe. His initial Apgar score was an eight. Five minutes later it was a nine. The nurse's smile behind her mask and her frequent nods of approval felt reassuring.

"Is he OK?" I mouthed to my son-in-law through the glass window.

He confidently bobbed his head up and down behind his own mask.

I'd always heard that C-section babies were particularly pretty. Now I could see for myself. Our two daughters had been born the more conventional way and had emerged red and wrinkled. Our older daughter Lindsay, after long hours of my labor and pushing, emerged with a cone-shaped head and forceps bruises on her temples. My good friend Donna was a nurse in OB at the time and was there when I delivered. Lindsay's head was so pointy that Donna covered it with a blanket before showing her to me. She later told Jay that she was afraid I'd be horrified if I saw how misshapen it looked. All I remember is seeing my new baby girl snugly wrapped in a blanket being held up next to me as I lay on the delivery table. I had no idea what that head looked like under the blanket, and luckily it improved in appearance before I found out.

Caden, on the other hand, looked absolutely beautiful. Without a single mark or discoloration, his skin glowed a soft, healthy pink. His dark eyes tried to focus on his daddy's face which gave him a puzzled expression suggesting he found this whole new experience of being in the world rather amazing. His head appeared free

7

of any lumps or indentations. No tight squeeze through the birth canal for him, lucky boy. Instead that head had been sheltered and protected for many months tucked right under his mommy's ribs.

In spite of his overall healthy appearance, however, I remained puzzled by how relaxed Caden looked. Most newborns I'd seen, including my own, were all scrunched up with arms and legs constantly in motion. Caden, lying there under the warming lights, looked like a sunbather on a Carolina beach. His arms and legs stretched outward, extending into such a relaxed pose that they barely moved at all. Caden seemed to be only slowly and gently awakening to this new world outside his mommy's tummy, and he certainly wasn't getting any too excited about the experience. That nagging feeling I had that Caden wasn't acting quite right for a newborn intensified.

I watched carefully as the nurse checked his startle reflex. Again I felt like his reaction just wasn't that strong. My own girls would startle so hard as newborns that they almost fell out of my arms if I wasn't careful. One time Jay was holding Lindsay up against his shoulder with one arm when he flipped the light switch with his other hand as he entered her bedroom. She startled so hard and arched her back so strongly at the click of the switch that he almost dropped her. Caden, on the other hand, seemed to barely move. Anxiously I searched the face of the nurse for any sign that she felt something was amiss. Although she repeated the test a couple of times, she didn't seem the least bit concerned with Caden's mild response. Before long he had his first bath, a quick swaddle, some suctioning of secretions from his mouth, and we were all off to a private room on the OB floor to reunite with Laurie.

When we arrived, Laurie was already settled comfortably in her bed. As the nurse placed Caden carefully into her arms, I grabbed the camera. Laurie and Zach created just the perfect picture of the proud new parents snuggling their newborn son. They looked over at me and smiled as I quickly snapped some pictures with my digital camera. Looking back at those pictures weeks later, I felt a pang of sadness, knowing those happy faces would soon become just a fleeting memory. At that particular instant, however, we had no idea what lay ahead. We were simply an ordinary, carefree, happy family enjoying one of life's special moments. Sadly, that picture proved to be a line in the sand: life before we knew and life thereafter.

"He's a little choky, which happens sometimes, especially with C-section babies," said the nurse. "I'll leave this bulb syringe, and if you need to, just suction his mouth out a bit. He seems a little floppy, but some babies just take some time to perk up. Don't worry," she called cheerfully over her shoulder as she breezed out of the room.

As Laurie held him, she too soon grew aware of Caden's raspy breathing. She used the bulb syringe to try and clear his mouth a bit while Zach hovered over them both. Readjusting Caden in her arms, she looked increasingly concerned.

Jay and I crowded around the bedside to get a closer look at Caden. I'd spent enough time staring at him from a distance, first through a nursery window and then across the bedside. Now I was eager to actually pick him up and cradle him in my arms.

"May I please hold him?" I asked.

I couldn't wait to give this baby his first Gramma kisses and rub my cheek against his soft, fuzzy head. Perhaps I even thought that I, an experienced mother, could hold him at a slightly different angle and correct that gurgling sound he continued to make. If only I'd known what was to come, what the next days and weeks would bring, I wouldn't have so thoughtlessly interrupted that mother-baby bonding time. In retrospect, I wish I had just left Caden in his mother's arms.

Standing by the bedside holding Caden, I also grew nervous with the noisy sounds of his breathing. After Zach unsuccessfully tried some more suctioning with the syringe, he rang for the nurse. Laurie looked worried, and I was beginning to feel very anxious myself. Why was he making that funny noise? What was wrong?

Hurrying into the room, the nurse peeked at Caden over my shoulder. Zach handed her the syringe, and she attempted to suction Caden herself.

"Let me just take him back to the nursery for a minute. I want to check his oxygen levels," she said matter-of-factly as she lifted him from my arms.

Turning, she walked quickly out of the room with him and disappeared down the hall.

Left alone together without the baby, the rest of us just stared helplessly at each other. Laurie looked like she was about to cry, and I felt like joining her. A feeling of panic rose in my throat, and my heart began to beat faster. That earlier sense of misgiving in my gut, that sense I had when I first saw Caden that something might be wrong, returned with a vengeance and grew ever sharper as the minutes passed. Unfortunately, those feelings would not be going away anytime soon.

The rest of that day melted into a blur of anxiety-ridden moments. Eventually the nurse returned and told us that Caden had been examined again and was being kept in the nursery for further observation. By a little after 7 AM, Dr. Lehrich, the pediatrician on duty, was notified of Caden's condition. Zach went to the nursery and stayed with Caden while Jay and I rotated back and forth between Laurie's bedside and Caden's, relaying updates between the two parents.

Laurie finally convinced the nurse to put her into a wheelchair and take her to the nursery so she could see Caden for herself. The nurses tried feeding Caden, both at Laurie's breast and with a bottle, but his suck was weak and his suck/swallow coordination poor. When he attempted to eat, he immediately choked, and his oxygen level desaturated.

By noon Caden was being considered for a possible move to the Special Care Nursery on another floor. Although Caden had spontaneous and symmetrical movement of both arms and both legs, he appeared very weak and lethargic. When a bed became available mid-afternoon, he was transferred upstairs for further evaluation; and Laurie was moved to a new room nearby.

Although we family members were blissfully unaware at the time, between 3:00 PM and 4:30 PM that first afternoon, Caden experienced four episodes of sleep apnea lasting thirty seconds. Each time the nurse was able to get him breathing again by patting him. "Vigorous tactile stimulation" is what the nurse's notes, which we read later, actually said. During those moments, his oxygen saturation dropped into the 65-72 percent range; and one time the nurse had to quickly administer some oxygen. These abnormal events obviously indicated some kind of problem, but no one had any answers.

In the afternoon Jay and I drove thirty minutes back to Laurie and Zach's house to tend to the dog and pick up some extra clothes for Zach. We returned to the hospital later that evening hoping for some good news. We didn't see Caden, as visitors were limited in the Special Care Nursery, but we did talk to Zach. Laurie, only a little more than twelve hours post-operative, was exhausted and frightened. Their pastor was with her, and the baby was still being closely monitored in the nursery, stable but unchanged. A consult with pediatric neurology had been ordered but would probably not take place until the next morning. Zach was just trying to hold things together.

"Mom, I don't know what to do," he said as the three of us huddled in the corridor outside the doors to the hospital floor where Caden and Laurie were resting.

"We just have to wait until morning, Zach. Maybe someone will know something then."

Zach's calling me Mom did not go unnoticed, and it touched my heart beyond words. Since he and Laurie had been married, he really hadn't settled on a name for me. I suggested that he call me Linda, Mom, or whatever he wanted, but for seven years he had managed to avoid calling me anything at all. Laurie always laughed that he was waiting until they had children so he could refer to me as Gramma. Now I realized that our relationship had changed overnight. I was no longer just an unnamed in-law but real family.

The next morning Caden remained a floppy, listless baby. His suck, swallow, and breathing were still abnormal. The good news was he continued to breathe on his own. As Jay and I arrived back at the hospital, however, preparations were being made to transfer both Laurie and Caden to Duke University Children's Hospital about an hour away in Durham.

Laurie had tried to spend some time that morning in the nursery where Zach had spent the night with Caden. Dr. Winchester from Raleigh Neurology had stopped by about 8:00 AM to examine Caden for a consult. Sitting together, she, Laurie, and Zach discussed her observations of Caden's condition. Dr. Winchester recommended a transfer to a larger hospital, and they chose Duke. With gentle thoroughness she outlined the type of diagnostic procedures they might expect once they arrived in Durham. The list was long, and at the time Laurie imagined it would take weeks or even months to complete. She had no idea what lay directly ahead.

Dr. March, Laurie's obstetrician, had heard about Caden's difficulties and stopped by to see how Laurie was doing. As Dr. Winchester questioned them both in detail about Laurie's pregnancy and Caden's delivery, he sat protectively with his arm around Laurie's shoulders.

"Laurie, I had no idea anything was wrong. There were no red flags during your pregnancy. Nothing to indicate a problem. I'm so, so sorry."

Obviously this kind man was just as stunned by Caden's condition as the rest of us. All the prenatal testing had been normal. The delivery had gone well. Caden had cried lustily at birth and seemed fine. Dr. March had left the operating room the day before thinking he had delivered a perfectly healthy baby boy. Now, he learned, something was most definitely wrong.

Before long Laurie's post-operative abdominal pain grew too severe, and she had to leave the nursery and return to her room. Upon our arrival at the hospital, Jay and I found her there in tears.

"Mom, I need to be with Caden, but it hurts too much to get out of bed," she sobbed.

I comforted her the best I could and tried to remain calm myself. I so wanted to erase the pain and fear I saw in her eyes. I was both terrified for my new grandson and also aching over my daughter's anguish, two emotions almost impossible to bear at once.

Suddenly the transfer team from Duke barged through her hospital room door, pushing the incubator containing Caden.

"Thought you might like to see your son before we take him," one medic said cheerfully.

Wow, I thought. What a kind gesture.

With tears trickling down her cheeks, Laurie reached over and softly touched Caden through the opening in the side of the transfer crib. She murmured a loving goodbye; and only when she said she was ready, did they roll him away. Immediately after they left, another medical team arrived, gave Laurie a shot of morphine, and readied her for her own trip to Duke by ambulance.

Zach gave Jay and me driving directions to the other hospital, and off we went. Scared, naive, and totally unprepared, we were about to enter the world of a big university teaching hospital. Even before we arrived, I sensed that our lives had been forever changed.

Chapter 2

"For I know the plans I have for you," declares the Lord,
"plans to prosper you and not to harm you,
plans to give you hope and a future."
Jeremiah 29:11

Laurie, still comfortably sedated, was settled in her room on the seventh floor by the time we arrived at Duke and tracked her down. Her nurse assured us she would sleep for a while, which was exactly what she needed. Jay and I set off to find Caden and Zach in the Neonatal Intensive Care Unit.

When we stepped off the elevator on the fifth floor, foreign territory awaited us. Like two frightened kindergarteners walking into school on the first day, we searched for the elusive entrance to the NICU. Little did we know that the maze of corridors we wandered uncertainly would soon become as familiar as our own front hallway at home.

About fifty yards ahead, we finally saw the sign for the NICU. Moving quickly in that direction, I noticed a small lounge to the left. Through the door I could see numerous chairs and recliners, a TV that no one seemed to be watching, and a sink and small refrigerator. The place looked dark and gloomy, and the smell of leftover pizza drifted out into the hall. Several people sat huddled under blankets, trying, I supposed, to get a little rest between crises. Later I discovered that whole families camped out there for days. They brought in their own carry-out or microwaveable food, pushed chairs together to form beds, and slept fitfully, waiting for more information from the doctors or nurses. In the future, when I sometimes dashed in there to wash my hands, I always left feeling like an eavesdropper on someone else's drama. The emotional tenor of the room was tangible and, depending on the latest medical update, seemed to alternate between a happy celebration and a wake.

Next to the lounge, we passed an activity room. I eventually learned that several afternoons a week, a lovely social worker named Grey provided various simple art projects as distractions for family members. How ironic that a woman named Grey would help to brighten our days. Under her direction, one afternoon Laurie and I each sat decorating an electrical outlet cover with printed paper and embellishments. She made hers for Caden's nursery at home, and I made mine for three-year-old granddaughter Cate's bedroom back in Maine. How we must have looked to others: this sad Mommy and Gramma hunched over a simple table, glue bottles in hands, struggling to erase, if just for a moment, the fear we carried. Time and again on one afternoon or another, we traded our sorrow for the comfort of that room, a sanctuary in which to pass the time while we waited in our own personal NICU uncertainty.

Coming to the actual NICU waiting room, I noticed how fairly small and sterile it felt. The walls were painted a sickly pinky peach. Straight back chairs with hard wooden arms and dull vinyl seats lined the perimeter. After spending first hours and then days sitting there, those seats would never feel any more comfortable than they looked that first afternoon. Several office doors opened off the area, and we watched quietly as various medical personnel came and went. On the opposite side of the waiting room was a tiny office with two plain desks, two swivel chairs, and two old beige computers. Although I didn't know it then, those computers would soon provide me an email lifeline to friends and family. The space itself eventually became my barren refuge. I went there to seek comfort and support from loved ones far away. Of greater importance, that room would be the place where I would first begin to tell Caden's story.

That first afternoon, we set up shop in one empty corner of the waiting room. We sat down in the exact same chairs we would return to day after day, like a family with their designated church pew. The few times we arrived and found our seats taken, we grudgingly moved to a different area. As soon as our chairs were vacant again, we quickly reclaimed them. That tiny semblance of routine provided some comfort and control in the chaotic place which for the time being comprised our whole world.

Across the room, a tall young guy with a loud, friendly voice sat behind a sliding glass window, giving visitors directions, answering questions, and unlocking the door to the inner sanctum where all the babies were kept. He seemed to know the regulars by sight and name and immediately clicked the doors open as they approached. Others he politely and patiently taught the rules of entry before sending them along their way back to their babies in the nursery. Across from the reception window was a closed door bearing the words "Family Room." Hmm, I wondered. Eventually I would find out the purpose for that room and politely look away when anyone entered or exited.

Other than those uncomfortable chairs, the main waiting area was starkly furnished. Ugly fluorescent lighting covered the ceiling like in an old-fashioned schoolroom, and a few stock pictures hung on the walls. I stared at those pictures every day for weeks, and yet I don't remember a single detail. One end table held some old magazines, and a small refrigerator had been thoughtfully filled with free bottled water. This strange, foreign space would quickly become our second home.

After a while, Zach exited the nursery to tell us we could go back into the NICU to see Caden. The nursery, however, had strict rules concerning visitors. Only the parents and pastor were permitted unlimited visitation. Zach and Laurie could also put six other people's names on an approved list, but only two visitors were allowed back with the baby at any one time. Zach let us go see Caden while he took a break.

The friendly guy at the desk buzzed Jay and me in through locked doors and quickly gave us a lesson in how to de-germ. He instructed us to wash our hands with a special soap for one full minute before thoroughly rinsing. A large, bold-faced clock hung over the sink to encourage compliance. Afterwards, we grabbed scrub gowns from an overhead cupboard and fumbled as we put them on for the first time. Over the next three weeks, we would repeat this procedure countless times a day whenever we re-entered the nursery. The Duke NICU could accommodate up to sixty-five critically ill newborns and infants, so the traffic in and out of that scrub room was nonstop. Dozens of those ugly, faded, blue print gowns lay neatly stacked in a high pile at the beginning of every day, and few were left by evening. God bless the housekeeping staff who tended the growing heap of discarded scrubs and replaced them each morning with a regular supply of freshly laundered ones. There were days when I went through four or five of those gowns myself.

Walking down the hall looking for Caden's room, I passed other dimly-lit cubicles with four to six bassinets each and one nurse for every two babies. All the rooms were fairly dark, in sharp contrast to the brightly-lit halls. The noise level was surprising. The constant hum of medical machines punctuated by the sharp ringing of alarms provided a cacophony of sounds that was anything but soothing. Monitors clicked and blinked while the nurses' voices hummed like bees. The sound that was most eerily missing, however, was that of the babies. Most of them were too sick or weak or small to even cry.

Entering Caden's room, Jay and I approached a nurse standing beside a warming bed in the far back corner. Caden was lying half naked in just his diaper with tubes, leads, and other unidentifiable medical devices attached to various parts of his tiny body. The monitor above his head recorded his fluctuating vital signs: heart rate, oxygen level, respiration rate, and temperature. The red and green lines seemed to jump all over the screen; and when his oxygen saturation dipped to an unsafe level, the alarm sounded. The nurse stayed close, and I appreciated her reassuring presence.

The other three bassinets in the room also held babies. One set of parents, definitely not newbies, was changing their little one's diaper like old pros. The baby right next to Caden looked huge in comparison to the rest. We found out later that he had been in the NICU ever since his birth about eighth months earlier. His occasional squall sounded like the bass section of the Mormon Tabernacle Choir compared to the barely audible whimpering of Caden. The fourth bed held a baby born very prematurely, her weight measured in ounces, not pounds. Compared to her, our Caden, who weighed six pounds and nine ounces, appeared ready to take on the world.

My first longing as I watched over Caden was to just stand there forever beside him. If I never moved, I thought, he would stay safe. If I just kept staring willfully at the monitors, they would continue to beep rhythmically. The constant presence of the nurses and other medical personnel was also oddly reassuring. We were at Duke, for heaven's sake. Surely here they could hand out a happy ending. Jay looked concerned but calm. I tried to be optimistic, but I felt like such a fake. Inside I was terrified.

Eventually we traded places with Zach, who had been patiently waiting his turn in the family lounge. Later we checked in on Laurie, who by then was awake and anxious to take her first wheelchair ride to the nursery to see her son. Shortly thereafter, Jay and I left the hospital for the long drive back to Clayton. How could it have been only twelve hours since we had gone to the Raleigh hospital that morning? Exhausted, we fell into bed, tearfully clung to each other, and prayed.

Chapter 3

"Do not fear; I will help you."
Isaiah 41:13

The next morning we dressed, gathered some clothes for Zach, who had slept at the hospital again, and drove back to Duke. The hour-long drive gave us time to talk and collect ourselves, but we were both very lost in our own thoughts. What would the day bring? How could this be happening? What should I be saying or doing that would be even a little bit comforting or helpful? I was usually a take charge person, but I felt totally out of control. Not knowing what to say or do next was very disconcerting.

After pulling into Duke's parking garage, we made our way through a tunnel beneath the street into the hospital and through a maze of corridors inside toward a large bank of elevators. Doctors, nurses, medical students, and the general public streamed along beside us in a steady early morning rush. Many wore white jackets or scrubs. Some wore business suits. Maintenance men were busy scraping and painting the walls in the hallway, and we carefully skirted their buckets and drop cloths. A few patients rolled along in wheelchairs or shuffled by trailing metal poles with hanging IV bags. Some people smiled and said good morning as they passed. Most were either distracted by the day's work to be done or wore expressions of fear and exhaustion mirroring our own.

The elevators filled quickly, but people politely held the door, stepped aside, and pushed the button when we called out the number for our floor. After exiting on the seventh level, we went looking for Laurie.

Sitting up in her bed, she still looked shell-shocked. Not only was she very sore from the recent C-section and her transfer to Duke the day before, but she was also busy learning how to use a breast pump. Caden's suck was too weak for nursing, so he had received a nasogastric (NG) tube and was getting his feedings through that. Laurie was providing nourishment by pumping every three hours. She had already taken a wheelchair ride to the NICU once with a delivery of breast milk, and Zach remained there with Caden, waiting for the doctors to make their morning rounds.

I looked at our beautiful daughter with fear and sorrow written all over her face. If only I could relieve you of your burden, I thought. The birth of her first child should have been a joyous occasion filled with photo opportunities and happy smiles all around. She should have been snuggled in her bed, nursing her happy and contented baby boy. Instead, here we all were, scared to death.

Remembering again her normal expressions of concern during her first pregnancy, I thought back to my casual reassurances. "All pregnant women worry," I had said. "Really, everything is going to be fine."

Now I felt like such a liar.

Jay and I left Laurie and went down to the fifth floor where we took our seats in the same corner of the NICU waiting room that we had occupied the day before. Other families were also gathering, and we found it impossible not to eavesdrop on their sad stories. Most memorable was a very young mother whose baby Tatiana had already been at Duke for several weeks. Her boyfriend, her own mother, and various other family members sat vigil with her. They took turns visiting with the baby and keeping each other company. This young woman looked like she should be preparing for her senior prom, not sitting in a NICU day after day. It soon became very apparent that Tatiana, who had been born prematurely in a hospital several hours away, had some very serious and life-threatening health issues. Clearly revealed in the conversation between the teenage mom and her own mother was the younger one's refusal to believe in the seriousness of her baby's condition. I understood her need to deny the facts; it still broke my heart to watch.

As Jay and I sat waiting, I wondered what Zach was hearing from Caden's doctors. When we arrived earlier, I saw them trooping past us into the nursery. The attending physician led the way, followed by fellows, residents, interns, medical students, and others whom I guessed to be specialists, a vast sea of white coats. Later I would learn their routine. A group of twelve to fifteen medical professionals with varying degrees of expertise and experience would crowd around a bassinet containing a sick baby. Usually one person did most of the talking. The rest listened, and many frantically scribbled notes on their clip pads. After completing their evaluation of one baby, they moved on to the next.

One day, after we had been at Duke for a while, I was standing by Caden's crib when all the alarms for the baby across the room sounded loudly. Within seconds a throng of medical professionals rushed into the room. Some began barking orders; others began performing procedures. As minutes passed, more personnel ducked their heads into the room to take a peek at this interesting case of a one-pound baby fighting for her life. Soon they left and returned to whatever else they had been doing. Just a moment's interruption adding a little excitement to an otherwise routine day. Please don't let Caden ever be viewed as just another learning experience or teachable moment, I silently prayed.

Sitting and waiting for updates on Caden was emotionally if not physically exhausting. Every muscle in my body felt tense as I struggled to relax and even my breathing. I tried to read, but my mind just wandered. Every so often I'd take a walk down the hall to the bathroom or the drinking fountain. There was a big aquarium near the elevators that provided an occasional distraction. Mindlessly watching fish swimming rhythmically back and forth proved oddly soothing. Across from the elevators was a large span of windows. Looking down from my spot on the fifth floor, I observed so many people rushing to and fro. Where were they going? Did they have a sick friend or family member inside? Were they taking a lunch break before returning to work? A small group of smokers tethered to their IV poles stood at the edge of the street. A discharged patient in a wheelchair sat hunched under a blanket, waiting to be picked up and driven home. How could the world possibly continue to spin while we sat waiting to find out what was wrong with our grandson? Slowly, I'd make my way back to the fifth floor to see if there were any updates on Caden's condition. Then I'd sit and wait some more.

Eventually Laurie returned to the nursery from her own room with her small vial of breast milk clutched in her hand. Not even really milk yet, the early colostrum would nourish Caden better than anything the hospital could provide. She and Zach spent most of the rest of that first afternoon in with Caden while Jay and I circulated back and forth, giving each other a turn by their side.

Meanwhile Caden was being poked and prodded and examined. The testing had begun in earnest, but any new information on his condition would probably not arrive until the next morning when the doctors made their rounds and reported the results. For the time being, he was stable.

By dinner, Jay and I were ready to head back to Clayton for the night. Leaving was difficult. Laurie wasn't being discharged until the next day, and Zach was staying another night at Duke with her and Caden. This was the day we all should have been going home together. When, I wondered, would that day come?

Chapter 4

"Do not be afraid of tomorrow. God is already there."
- Unknown

Our first few days of NICU life soon settled into a familiar routine. While Laurie was still in the hospital recovering, Zach slept in her room. Jay and I drove back to Clayton every evening, trying to time our forty-five-mile drive to avoid the Raleigh rush hour traffic. In the morning, we returned to the hospital, eager for any updates. Zach, Laurie, Jay, and I rotated in and out of Caden's room throughout the day in pairs. Every three hours, Laurie went down the hall and around the corner to the private nursing room to fill her bottles with mother's milk. When we weren't with Caden, we sat and tried to distract ourselves with conversation, reading, and email. Hour after hour, we waited impatiently for test results and updates.

The tests on Caden, begun immediately after his arrival at Duke, continued. Many different doctors examined him, and the techs continually drew blood. Eventually a tech inserted a line in Caden's umbilical cord so he would not have to stick him every time more blood was needed. Unfortunately, this meant Caden couldn't be easily held because if the line became dislodged, he could bleed to death. Some of his blood was sent off to the Mayo Clinic to be screened for various genetic abnormalities. Those test results could take weeks. Other blood, including some from Laurie and Zach, was shipped to another genetics lab in Wisconsin. Scientists miles away would search to find the answer to Caden's difficulties, a thought that was simultaneously comforting and terrifying. No part of his body seemed off limits for probing, scoping, or scanning. In addition to all the blood work, he had a brain ultrasound and MRI, a lung x-ray, an echocardiogram, and an ultrasound of his kidneys. Nothing seemed to be left unexamined. He was checked and rechecked and checked again.

The speech therapist quickly ordered a swallow study and an examination by an ENT. Initial findings seemed encouraging. Though weak, Caden was able to suck and swallow. He also definitely had a gag reflex. The therapist assured us he should eventually be able to eat and drink normally. In days, months, or years? Too soon to tell.

Knowing all the procedures that Caden was undergoing, some painful and many at the very least uncomfortable, was hard on all of us. He was such a tiny, helpless baby. He shouldn't have to experience all this suffering so early in his life. With his umbilical venous catheter in place, we couldn't even hold him regularly to give him some comfort. All we could do was stroke his little body and murmur soothing words. It didn't seem like nearly enough. Zach stood faithfully by Caden's side as every procedure took place, and, better than any of us, he deciphered the medical terminology and made sense of the results. We clung to every bit of positive news like a lifeline.

Caden's respiration and oxygen levels remained uneven, and his monitors continued to beep way too often for any of us to feel at ease. To stimulate his breathing, he was treated with a daily dose of caffeine, which seemed to be helping. Nevertheless, as I stood by his bassinet I constantly eyed the monitors indicating his oxygen saturation. Staring so hard at that machine, I willed those numbers to stay in the high nineties. Mostly I worried that if I looked away, the numbers would fall and the beeping would begin again. We all lived in fear that at some point we would enter the nursery and find him on a ventilator.

When tests of Caden's spine revealed no abnormalities, a neurology tech tested the nerve impulses running down Caden's arms and legs by means of an electromyogram (EMG). He wanted to verify that the nerves in Caden's arms and legs were working properly and that the junctures between the nerves and the muscles were healthy. Surely this test had to have hurt Caden, but sadly it had to be done anyway. Yes, the tech discovered, the nerves were doing their job stimulating the muscles. After each test, Zach came to the waiting room to update the rest of us on the results. Meanwhile, I tried not to think about how painful some of those tests probably were for our sweet baby boy.

Cardiologists, pulmonologists, urologists, neurologists: all searched for a medical explanation for Caden's condition. Test results and blood work, however, continued to come back with normal findings. The consensus was that the issue appeared to be neuromuscular. If the brain, spinal cord, and nerves seemed to be functioning properly, then the problem must reside within the muscles themselves. The pediatric neurologist scheduled a muscle biopsy for Friday.

While all the testing was going on, we as a family had been trying to regain some sense of control over our lives. Laurie had transitioned from the wheelchair to a painful shuffle. Sometimes she was there with Caden for his tests, but often she was off pumping her milk. Her hours seemed divided between Caden's bedside and the private nursing room down the hall. Wanting and needing to be in two places at the same time left her feeling extremely frustrated. In addition, she felt weak and uncomfortable as she slowly recovered from her abdominal surgery. Her hormones swung widely, and she certainly wasn't getting the rest she required. I worried about her as much as Caden. In spite of everything, she focused on the needs of Caden and soldiered on.

Zach had taken on the role of father bear to his cub. Most of the day he stood at Caden's bedside, murmuring, whispering, and touching him soothingly. Caden never failed to respond. At the sound of Zach's voice, Caden's blood pressure steadied and his respiration and oxygen levels normalized. He knew his daddy. The doctors made rounds daily, but the exact time fluctuated. Zach always arrived early in the nursery and waited patiently to get the latest updates on Caden's condition.

As a biologist himself, his scientific training proved enormously helpful. He knew the questions to ask, and he understood the complexity of the answers. He pushed for details as needed, and evaluated recommended procedures. Zach was Caden's best advocate and a medical interpreter for the rest of us.

Jay and I tried to function as the support team, but the assignment was daunting and our skills lacking. Though he hid his feelings well, Jay was more distraught than I had ever seen him. He so wanted to fix everything, to make it all right. He could hardly bear the pain in his "little girl's" eyes or the suffering of his grandson. If only he could have been the one poked and prodded, scoped and scanned, he would gladly have taken Caden's place.

"I would give my life if it meant that little boy could be perfectly healthy," he confided one night. His heart was breaking and so was mine.

Born and raised in a small town in Ohio, I come from a long line of devout Lutherans. Members of my family, myself included, have attended Trinity Lutheran Church in Ashland, Ohio, for five generations, and we were active Lutherans. We taught Bible School, served on building committees, cooked in the church kitchen, prepared food for funeral lunches, and belonged to women's circles and share groups. My mother was employed as the church secretary for fifteen years, and my sister Diane worked for five years as the church's Christian Education Coordinator. She and I both completed five year terms on the church council. Our children sang in the choirs as we had done before them. I knit prayer shawls, helped lead a book study, and attended adult Sunday school classes. Jay also served as a regular lector and usher at Sunday services.

Obviously, I was raised in a family with a strong and abiding faith. Some of my earliest childhood memories are of going to Sunday School and Vacation Bible School with my friends and sisters. We said prayers before meals and at bedtime. I fondly remember my mother reading bedtime stories to me from one of my favorite Golden Books: "Daniel and the Lion's Den," "Joseph and His Coat of Many Colors," "Moses and the Bulrushes." She also played "Jesus Loves Me" and many of her own favorite hymns on the piano while my sisters and I snuggled beside her on the piano bench waiting for Dad to come home from work at the end of the day. We went to church as a family every Sunday. I learned very early in my life to believe in a loving God and to have faith in His protection and grace.

With Caden's birth, however, my faith was being sorely tested. I prayed fervently that he would survive. I prayed that whatever was wrong with him wasn't serious. I prayed that if it was serious, it could be cured. I prayed for comfort for Laurie and Zach. I prayed for strength and courage and endurance for us all. Sometimes I strongly felt God's presence by my side. Sometimes I felt very much alone.

Jay often prayed aloud for Caden. He prayed at his bedside, in the waiting room, and in the car driving to and from the hospital. Before we went to sleep every night, he steadfastly prayed for Caden's healing. I loved hearing him pray. The rich, deep timbre of his voice was soothing and reassuring. Jay believed in miracles and felt Caden would be healed. His voice strongly expressed that conviction.

I admit I often had misgivings about a total healing. I knew God had the power to heal Caden immediately, but I certainly didn't know if He would. I struggled with what my prayers should say, momentarily forgetting that God already knew my heart's desire. Maybe, I thought, we should be giving God options instead of directives. I questioned the content of our prayers not because I had lost faith in God's abilities, but because I didn't know how to respond if God's answer was no. "What ifs" filled my head, crowding out any sense of inner peace. My faith felt so weak and my need so great.

Still, Jay and I continued our prayers for strength, for understanding, for courage, for a miracle. I remembered reading somewhere that we pray, not to change God's mind, but to change our own. We prayed to feel God's presence; but in our humanness, we also wanted answers. Deep inside we knew those answers might not be what we hoped for, but we weren't yet ready to face that possibility.

Chapter 5

"Is any one of you sick? He should call the elders of the church to pray over him and anoint him with oil in the name of the Lord. And the prayer offered in faith will make the sick person well; the Lord will raise him up."
James 5:14-15

Although I had been raised as a Lutheran, Jay grew up in the Greek Orthodox tradition with very devout parents and grandparents. His sister Irene told me that most Greek families kept holy oil in their homes to use with a blessing over anyone who was sick or going through a difficult time. Traditionally, the oil was olive oil which had been blessed by the local priest. Jay remembered his Aunt Cora's father, a highly respected and beloved priest, giving Jay's mother some holy oil, which she used in their home when Jay was growing up. Irene encouraged us to get some oil, pray over it, and then use it to make the sign of the cross on Caden's forehead as we said a blessing over him.

Friday morning Jay and I stopped at Walgreens on the way to the hospital and bought a travel size bottle of baby oil.

"Dear, God," we prayed in the car, "we don't know the proper words to turn this into holy oil, but we believe in Your greater power and ask You to bless this oil. May it bring a miracle of healing to Caden. Amen."

Arriving at Duke, we made our way to the now familiar NICU. Laurie was scheduled for discharge later that day; and when we got there, she was off pumping her milk. Zach had gone to pick up a prescription at the hospital pharmacy and to make arrangements to rent a breast pump to use at home. Jay and I set up camp in our customary corner of the waiting room.

When Laurie returned with her milk, she and Jay went back to the nursery to check on Caden. While they were there, Jay took out the oil, and he and Laurie anointed Caden and prayed over him. They did it as an act of faith, a means of showing our belief that Caden was a special child of God. God loved him and would protect him always. He would heal Caden according to His plan and in His time. Our job was to trust and be patient.

Caden's doctors had already made their rounds by the time we arrived. They told Zach that the surgical team would try to fit Caden into the surgery schedule later that afternoon for a muscle biopsy. Examining a piece of his muscle would hopefully provide a diagnosis. The muscle biopsy would require putting Caden under general anesthesia. Unfortunately, with his poor muscle tone, he was at high risk for breathing problems and difficulty coming out of anesthesia. Worst case scenario, he might be on a ventilator for a while. Otherwise, the procedure should be fairly simple. The surgeon planned to remove a piece of muscle from Caden's right thigh. If necessary, he might also have to take some from his left thigh. Those biopsies would be examined later in the lab under a microscope. Any irregularities would be noted, and the results should be available in a few days. Caden's thigh would carry a large scar. At least on a guy, I thought, scars are considered cool and could provide him bragging rights in the future. I was trying so hard to remain positive.

By this time, Jay and I had discovered the Ronald McDonald room on the pediatric wing of the fifth floor. Made up of three cozy little rooms, this space provided a peaceful escape for exhausted families. There were computers to use, free snacks and drinks available, and even access to laundry and shower facilities. A plate of homemade cookies and brownies always sat in the middle of a small kitchen table. Jay and I became regular visitors, and that Friday we walked over for a mid-afternoon break while Laurie and Zach sat with Caden awaiting his surgery.

As we returned to the waiting room about twenty minutes later, Caden's nurse Marie approached us.

"Laurie and Zach would like you to come back with Caden," she said.

Something must be wrong, I thought.

"Is everything okay?" I asked hopefully.

"Just come on back with me," Marie replied, politely ignoring the concern in my voice.

When we got back to Caden's room, Laurie was sitting in a chair holding him. Except for the nasal tube and the various wires emerging from beneath his baby blanket, he snuggled in her arms like any contented, sleeping newborn. Zach and the lead pediatric neurologist in the NICU hovered nearby talking quietly. Seeing the tears running down Laurie's cheeks, I knew something was very wrong.

"What's the matter?" I could hear the frantic edge in my own voice as I searched faces for answers.

The doctor began to speak. His exact words blurred as I struggled to pay attention while not taking my eyes off Caden.

"The geneticist was just here . . . might live a month or two . . . perhaps in a wheelchair or on a vent."

My mind struggled to make sense of his words.

"I'm so sorry," he said, and then he turned and walked away.

This can't be happening, I thought. I picked Caden up out of Laurie's arms and took her place in the chair. Looking down at Caden's sweet face, I refused to believe what I had just heard. Despite the doctor's grim prognosis, so many test results so far had been encouraging. He also seemed to be getting a tiny bit stronger every day and had still not needed any breathing assistance. Weren't those all good signs? I wondered. Surely this baby was not going to die. The stricken looks on Laurie's and Zac's faces were painful to watch.

"I don't care what they say. I refuse to believe that my little boy is going to die," cried Laurie.

I marveled at her spirit. Although I had always viewed Laurie as the emotionally fragile one of our two daughters, I sensed now that she was much stronger than even she knew.

As the significance of the doctor's words began to sink in, Zach whispered to me, "Mom, what should we do? What if they're right?"

I remember answering, "Then we take him home and love him." But none of us was ready to give up.

Soon word came down from surgery that the team had run out of time. The muscle biopsy was postponed until Monday. Disappointed as we were, Jay suggested to the doctor who had returned to deliver the news that perhaps a delay could be a blessing. After enduring so many tests and procedures over the last four days, maybe Caden would be rested and stronger after the weekend. The doctor just nodded and looked away.

"You don't think he'll be any better by Monday, do you?" I asked.

"No," he replied.

We took turns holding our precious Caden and even took some pictures. I tried to memorize every second he was in my arms. That beautiful skin, those tiny lips forming that perfect bow of a mouth. So tiny. So vulnerable. We were not giving up on this little guy. He was our angel, and God had surely given him to us for a reason.

Finally Zach spoke up, "No matter what happens, he is the perfect child for us, and we are the perfect parents for him. Someday we'll run together; and if that means I push him in a wheelchair, then that's what I'll do."

How certain I felt at that moment that my daughter and my grandson had the right man loving them.

The surgeon and anesthesiologist stopped by later to apologize for the postponed surgery. They assured us they'd be back on

Monday. Their kindness and compassion stood in stark contrast to the earlier doctor's matter-of-fact pronouncements. Jay asked if they would join us in prayer. The nurse laid her hand gently on Jay's shoulder, and all of us reached out to put our hands on Caden. Jay prayed fervently for healing for Caden, for guidance and skill for the doctors, and for strength and trust for the rest of us. I was so touched by the doctors and nurse praying with us. For the first time all afternoon, I felt a little of God's comfort and peace wash over me.

Reluctantly, we returned Caden to his warming bed under the watchful eye of Marie.

"This baby has made some tiny improvements this week," she said. "He's breathing on his own. I've seen a lot of babies, and the doctors aren't always right. Don't give up!"

With heavy hearts we left the room, and for the first time since Caden's birth, we all headed home to Clayton together. Jay and I were driving our car, and Laurie and Zach were in theirs. The ride was very quiet as Jay and I both found ourselves lost in thought. Anyone who knows me well, knows I tend to process my thoughts in a crisis by either writing or talking, but at that moment I was truly at a loss for words.

Earlier in the afternoon, however, before we left the hospital, I sent out the following email:

Dear Family and Friends,

We are very scared and discouraged. Although Caden appears to be holding his own, his condition is critical. His surgery never took place because, after waiting all day, they weren't able to fit him into the surgical schedule. So he is now on the list for Monday for his muscle biopsy.

A geneticist who had never seen him before looked at him today and gave a very poor prognosis: severely handicapping or fatal. We felt that was a bit premature without the biopsy or genetic test results, but it is difficult to overlook the words of an expert.

I think that because all the tests so far have been normal, they feel his condition must be extremely rare and serious. We aren't giving up hope on our precious little guy, but we're in so much pain.

Now I sat in the car next to Jay, the comfort of his hand in mine. With tears filling my eyes and spilling down my cheeks, I couldn't think of a single thing to say. Actually, I wanted Jay to do the talking. I wanted to hear strength and reassurance in his voice. I wanted him to make the pain and fear go away. But he was equally devastated, and at the moment he just couldn't be the person I wanted. No one could.

Though I was unable to speak, thoughts of our family raced through my mind. Jay and I have two grown, married daughters. Lindsay lives in Maine with her husband Rick and our little granddaughter Cate. Their house is just down the private road from ours, and we see them almost daily. Right then they seemed painfully far away.

Laurie is the younger sister. As a child, she was the one who made us laugh with her silly faces and poses. She also brought out my most tender, maternal feelings when she snuggled in my lap with her blankie in her hand and her thumb in her mouth. Laurie laughs and cries easily, sometimes within the same few moments. She is a perfectionist, who works harder than most for everything she does. She's a list maker and an organizer. She makes friends easily. People like her. She hates change. Constancy in her life is her security. Anxiety is her constant companion. She is the daughter I worry about most. Why had this happened to her?

When we all got home, Laurie immediately called Matt Evans, their good friend and pastor of Greater Heights United Methodist Church in Clayton. When Matt arrived, Jay and I retreated to the den to give them some privacy. Through the closed doors we couldn't make out their words, but we could still hear the anguish in their voices.

I felt so grateful that Laurie and Zach had Matt and their church friends and their neighbors for help and support during these difficult days. Amy, who lived next door, was arranging for evening meals and caring for their dog. She and her husband Aaron even took care of some expensive car repairs for Laurie and Zach in the weeks that followed. Scott and Sarah, neighbors on the other side, were also available with comfort and encouragement. Scott had arranged and paid for Laurie and Zach's house to be power washed because he knew they had been wanting to have that done before Caden was born. This thoughtfulness was only the beginning of the many acts of kindness that would pour in for weeks and months to come.

While Jay and I sat in the den, something in the corner of the room caught my eye. When we had left home in Maine to drive to North Carolina for Caden's birth, we had loaded the car with some of the baby items Cate had outgrown, in particular a disassembled ExerSaucer. Now there it sat, almost too painful to look at. Would Caden ever be able to use it? Would he ever sit, stand, or play in it? I felt like the toy was mocking us. Surprised, I watched as Jay dragged it to the center of the room and began putting the pieces together. What was he thinking?

"What are you doing?" I asked in confusion.

"Someday my grandson will play in this," he replied. The determination in his voice was palpable. His confidence encouraged me. I joined him on the floor and picked up one of the parts. With tears trickling down our faces, we assembled Caden's ExerSaucer. Nobody was giving up yet.

Chapter 6

"Therefore do not worry about tomorrow,
for tomorrow will worry about itself.
Each day has enough trouble of its own."
Matthew 6:34

The rest of the weekend passed in a blur. Zach's parents, Belva and Gerry, and his sister Alisson drove over thirteen hours from their homes in Bowling Green, Ohio, to North Carolina to see their new grandson and nephew. Very faith-filled people, they brought with them a sense of hope and confidence in the power of God and prayer that was encouraging. I envied their conviction.

They spent all their time at the hospital where Jay and I saw them briefly on Saturday. By Sunday afternoon they were headed back to Ohio and their full-time jobs. Part of me wished I could join them. To be able to leave the NICU and maybe get a break from all that was happening would have provided a welcome respite. I knew from experience that if I wasn't physically present during a family crisis, I could temporarily go into a bit of denial mode and just ignore the situation. On the other hand, who was I kidding? Leaving wouldn't eliminate the worry, only magnify it. Thankfully I had the option of remaining in North Carolina because there was nowhere else I could have imagined being. I was right where I was needed. Right where I belonged.

On Saturday I talked to my sister Diane, who lives with her family back in my hometown in Ohio. I am the oldest of the three of us, and Diane is the youngest. Our middle sister Kathy moved to California years ago, but Diane and I had both lived in our hometown of Ashland for most of our lives until Jay and I had retired to Maine the previous year. We had raised our children together, vacationed together, and cared for our ailing parents together. We had celebrated life's high points and consoled each other during life's struggles. Our husbands claim they can't tell our voices apart on the phone. We have unknowingly bought each other the same birthday cards. I was present in the delivery room when her middle child Jamie was born. She sneaked into the hospital after hours when I gave birth to our first daughter Lindsay. We are sisters and the best of friends. She is the one I call when life is good, and the one I call when life is falling apart.

Her voice on the other end of the phone provided a needed lifeline when she called me that weekend. As soon as we said hello, we were both in tears. I sat on the front porch steps of my daughter's house with the warm, early spring Carolina sun shining down on me, and I sobbed. Although a lot of our conversation centered on the details of Caden's condition and his upcoming biopsy, I also poured out my fears and sadness. Our mother had passed away just five months earlier. My grief was still raw, and I missed her terribly.

"I miss Mom so much," I cried. "I keep thinking if she were here, she would know what to do. She would tell me how to live through this experience. I'm sixty years old, and I want my mom."

"She's with you, you know," Diane soothed.

"I know. I feel her presence. I feel like she's in my head. I guess I do know what she would say if she were here; I know she would expect me to be calm and brave."

"She's watching over you," Diane said. "And if the worst happens, she'll be waiting for Caden in Heaven."

I thought of my other sister Kathy's recent email, "Linda, you are having to be strong right now. Mom would be so proud of you."

And another email from our friend Chris also touched my heart, "God will keep you strong. Linda, sometimes I think about your mom and what she would advise – such a strong and wise lady. May you find strength thinking of her."

Yes, I knew Mom would tell me to stay strong. Furthermore, she would have urged me to remain positive and expect the best possible outcome. For now, Caden was holding his own, and she would have reminded me to cling to that knowledge with hope and confidence. My mom was not a stoic. In the face of difficult times, she often resorted to a good cry. Afterward, however, she wiped her eyes, put a smile on her face, and decided how to handle whatever lay ahead. Now she would expect the same response from me. More importantly, she would believe I could do it. At times I could almost hear her voice in my head: *He's not giving up and neither should you. Wait and see what the test results show. Don't borrow trouble.* My mom always had a good saying for every situation and remembering that made me smile. When I hung up the phone, I felt more peaceful than I had since our heartbreak began.

On Sunday Laurie was able to do what the nurses called "kangaroo care." She sat in a chair next to Caden's crib and held him against her chest, bare skin to bare skin. As she cuddled him for two straight hours, all his vital signs stayed within the normal range. His blood pressure stabilized, and his oxygen saturation level held right in the desired ninety-five to one hundred percent level. The monitors remained blissfully silent. Sitting nearby, I watched them both sleeping peacefully: my exhausted daughter and her precious baby boy. Caden's chest rose and fell evenly beneath the blanket over his back as she held him next to her heart. How beautiful the power of a mother's love.

As the weekend drew to a close, we knew many challenges lay ahead. First would be the muscle biopsy the next morning. We all now believed that that would give us the answers we were looking for. The doctors had tried to prepare us for the worst, but we had had a few days to get over the shock of their prognosis, and we were nowhere ready to concede defeat. Caden seemed to be a fighter too. With God's help, we were expecting a victory.

Chapter 7

"Be strong and take heart, all you who hope in the Lord."
Psalm 31:24

As we drove back to the hospital together on Monday morning, our thoughts focused ahead on the day's surgery. Caden's condition had remained stable throughout the weekend. He had developed a little jaundice and spent most of Saturday and Sunday under the ultraviolet lights. I had to smile at how peaceful and relaxed he looked stretched out in his diaper, wearing his little sunglasses. Basking contentedly in his own specialized, artificial sunlight, he obviously was leaving it to the rest of us to do all the worrying.

One of our ongoing frustrations concerned Caden's feeding and weight. The doctors wanted him to show slow gains. That said, when Caden had a procedure, the nurses often had to withhold his feeding for long periods. He had not been fed for over twelve hours on Friday while he waited for his biopsy, which then never happened. By Monday morning he again had not been fed since midnight in preparation for his rescheduled surgery. How can he gain weight and get stronger, we wondered, if he isn't able to eat? Anger and frustration fueled our worry. Just a week ago we had been joyously celebrating this precious child's birth. Now we feared for his very life.

Caden's weak muscle tone made his surgery extra risky. The anesthetic posed the greatest danger. Once ventilated, would Caden have trouble being weaned from the breathing machine when the surgery was over? The doctors warned us that the elimination of respiratory support might be difficult and require a very gradual withdrawal over an extended period of time. This news alarmed us beyond words. We had taken such comfort in Caden's ability to breathe adequately on his own. Despite the frequent rise and fall of his oxygen saturation levels, he had not needed any mechanical breathing assistance since his admission to Duke. The nurses had continued to give him just the small dose of caffeine each day to provide a little respiratory stimulation. Now we wondered if that would remain enough. The words of the geneticist, "possibly vent dependent," slipped into my mind.

Throughout the previous week, Zach and I had each spent our spare moments researching various muscle myopathies (diseases). Many had terrible prognoses. Some of the more common, and less severe, were quickly eliminated by the negative results of the initial testing done on Caden. Zach grew increasingly discouraged, and I began to realize that his fears were based on the horrible outcomes of most of the other possible diagnoses that remained.

Laurie and Jay, however, stayed focused on the immediate concerns of the day. They refused to discuss or even consider what the future might hold. Zach and I, on the other hand, turned again and again to our research: facts and science. This was natural for Zach because of his training. I did it looking for answers so I could feel more in control. If I could just understand what was going on with Caden, if I could just put a name to it, I'd be able to wrap my mind around the consequences and begin to cope. Or so I thought. Not knowing what we were dealing with was driving me crazy. Hopefully this biopsy would give us some answers and reveal Caden's specific condition. The very real possibility that we might never know for sure what was wrong with Caden was just too much for me to even consider.

Jay continued to cope by seeking strength in his prayers, his faith, and the possibility of a miracle. I witnessed that and tried to share in his confidence. I too believed in miracles, and I think I prayed just as passionately. Sometimes I really did feel God's presence there in the NICU, but I still had a knot in the pit of my stomach most of the time.

Caden finally went into surgery later that morning. The anesthesiologist, who had stopped by to check on Caden before he went to pre-op, joined together with all of us as we prayed for the operation to go well. With heads bowed and hands held tightly, we encircled Caden's crib. Jay fervently lifted his voice, asking for God's protection of Caden and for skill on the part of the doctors and nurses who would perform the surgery. Some of the nurses in the room quietly came over, laid their hands on our shoulders, and echoed our *Amen*. Tears sprang to my eyes at the kindness shown by these strangers and at the support of our faith that they offered so freely. No sooner had Jay finished his prayer than the staff pushed Caden's crib out of the room and wheeled our baby down the hall away from us.

During the operation, the surgeon carefully removed a good size chunk of muscle from Caden's tiny right thigh. Later in the lab, that specimen would be carefully examined under a microscope for any irregularities of the muscle, and in a few days we hoped to have some answers. The surgery itself went well, though the anesthesiologist later told us he had some difficulty intubating Caden, a situation which then required him to use a slightly different method. That change in plans turned out to be a blessing in disguise. Caden emerged from recovery without a vent and was breathing on his own as he was taken back to the nursery.

The expression of relief on Zach's face when he came into the waiting room to update Jay and me reassured us that Caden was fine. Jay and I had spent our time during the surgery alternately praying, fidgeting, and pacing. Now my heart felt a little lighter, and tears of relief filled my eyes. We would have to wait a few days for the results of the muscle biopsy, but for now our little guy was out of surgery and breathing well. Our prayers had been answered. Life seemed just a bit less grim for the moment, and I went off to the computer room to email the good news to family and friends. Zach returned to the nursery to be with Caden and Laurie. Jay sat down to catch his breath.

Over the previous weekend, Bill, a very dear friend, had generously offered his frequent flier miles to our daughter Lindsay so she could fly from Maine to Raleigh to see her new nephew and the rest of us. Laurie and Lindsay were close sisters, and I knew Lindsay's presence would offer Laurie comfort and support. A high school biology teacher, Lindsay, like Zach, had a science background; she too had been researching possible diagnoses. I was anxious to hear her thoughts on Caden's condition. Most of all, I would just be happy to have her near. This was a family crisis, and we all needed each other for strength and comfort. I knew we could all benefit from Lindsay's optimistic nature and cheerful disposition. I had just about cried myself dry, and I needed my other daughter to boost my spirits. Thankfully, she would be arriving the next day.

Throughout the week since Caden's birth, I reflected on Laurie's recent pregnancy, wondering what signs we might have missed that something could be wrong with Caden. I remembered her ultrasound at about eighteen weeks when they had learned they were having a boy. Everything had looked perfectly fine. Several weeks of secretly discussing possible names ensued. Finally one night they called us to announce they had decided to name their son Caden Zachary. Zach told us that *Caden* meant "strong warrior." I loved the name but had no idea at the time how fitting it would be. Now others were also noticing the significance of his name.

My sister-in-law Irene had just emailed me the Bible verse Isaiah 43:1: "Fear not, for I have redeemed you; I have called you by name; you are mine."

My friend JoEllen wrote, "I looked up *Caden,* and it is taken from the name *Cadell* which means 'spirit of battle, warrior, companion, fighter.' He certainly fits his name."

46

From lifelong friend Pam came this encouragement, ". . . our little 'warrior'! Look how much power one little guy has. He is controlling a world of friends who wake up every morning searching for positive progress. He has already made a difference and he is only a few days on this side!"

Jake, a former student of mine and close friend of Laurie and Zach's, sent these words, "I do believe that each of us was made just as God intended, all of us unique, and I believe that God has created Caden for a specific plan and purpose. He has been fearfully and wonderfully made in God's likeness (Psalm 139)."

My friend Katherine wrote that she and her husband and their three children had planted a flower garden at their home in Florida and erected a sign which said, "Caden's Garden." Along with her note, she sent a beautiful picture of all the flowers in bloom. What a thoughtful gesture.

Friends and family were reaching out with so much love and support. In ways they couldn't possibly realize, they were lifting my spirits and helping me to stay strong.

On Tuesday I sent out an email updating everyone on Caden's progress after his surgery:

> Caden did very well through the night. His blood pressure is down and when the pediatric neurologist was asked about a possible kidney scan, he said, "Who on earth told you that?"
>
> Caden's pain is minimal (they were able to get enough tissue out of just one thigh), so they've only had to use Tylenol. He is bright-eyed and alert. They did a brain MRI this morning. The brain ultrasound was normal but this is more thorough. Since the day shift arrived, they have not had to suction his throat.
>
> Some of you may think I'm crazy, but I told Jay I think God's hand was at work yesterday in the OR. The anesthesiol-

ogist told us there was a strong to probable possibility that Caden would be intubated and come back from surgery on a vent. Funny how they couldn't get the tube down his throat (they said because of secretions), and he came through it fine breathing on his own. Today the secretions are better. Praise God.

Later that afternoon Laurie again did kangaroo care with Caden. First, she settled herself comfortably in the chair at Caden's bedside. Then the nurse had Laurie remove her shirt and lay Caden, dressed in just his diaper, on her chest, bare skin to bare skin. Tucking a blanket around them both, she left them to snuggle in silence. In moments they were both fast asleep. I watched as Caden's monitors quietly resumed a normal rhythm. No beepers going off; no numbers outside the normal range. The power of a mother's touch was amazing to witness.

After a few hours, Laurie and Zach headed home a little early to beat the rush hour traffic. It was always hard to leave Caden at the end of each day, but Laurie, especially, really needed the break. Her recovery from her C-section was going slowly, and she was exhausted. Sleeping each night in her own bed was comforting despite the long drives back and forth to the hospital each day. Jay and I stayed behind to sit with Caden for a while longer since we were planning to pick Lindsay up at the airport around seven on our way home. Feeling a bit restless after Laurie and Zach left, I went over to Caden's nurse who was sitting at the computer.

"Excuse me. I was just wondering. Have the results of Caden's brain MRI returned?"

She pulled up some information on her screen.

"Yes, but I'm not allowed to give you the results. I didn't tell you anything; however, read right here," she said, pointing to the screen.

I scanned the page until my eyes fell on the words, "Brain MRI: Normal." My knees felt weak as a huge sense of relief washed over me. No matter what else was wrong, our baby boy could think normally. He could learn. He could understand. Those eyes staring up at us so intently each day were as alert and aware as we thought. Tears filled my eyes. One big victory; one day at a time.

Jay and I left the hospital that evening with smiles on our faces. After picking up Lindsay at the Raleigh airport, we three headed to Laurie and Zach's house in Clayton. I couldn't wait to share the good news about Caden's MRI with Laurie and Zach. We all enjoyed our evening together. Lindsay's upbeat attitude and sense of humor, along with Caden's good test results, provided just the right remedy for our fear and fatigue. At least for one evening, life seemed a bit more hopeful.

Chapter 8

"Give thanks to the Lord, for He is good;
his love endures forever."
Psalm 118:1

Early the next morning, all five of us headed back to Duke. Lindsay finally got to meet her new little nephew. I think she got a kick out of being Aunt Lindsay for the first time. Having the opportunity to hold and cuddle this precious new member of our family was a moment for her to treasure. Trying to give her as long as possible with Caden and Laurie, I retreated to the waiting room and busied myself on the computer.

I sent out my daily email update, noting Lindsay's arrival and Caden's continuing progress. Some encouraging improvements had occurred. Although Caden was always kept tightly swaddled, I noticed him squirming around much more like a typical baby. He wasn't lying quite so still as he had been right after birth. When Laurie changed his diaper earlier that morning, he had pulled his legs up, and when she pulled them down to fasten his diaper, he had pulled them back up again. Far different from those listless legs of a week ago. Also that morning, under the supervision of the speech therapist, he had taken an ounce of breast milk from a bottle, and he had burped. Who would have thought a burp could prompt so many smiles? Consequently, he had been approved for oral feeding five times a day. The breast milk would first be offered in a bottle. What he didn't consume by mouth would then be given through the NG tube. A tiny step, for sure, but a step in the right direction.

Other accomplishments had occurred as well. When I went back to the nursery to take my turn with Caden, I found him lying on his side in his bassinet sucking loudly on his pacifier. The nurse responded to my raised eyebrows, "Sucking his paci like a big boy."

He was also coughing, yawning, scrunching up his face if disturbed, and crying a bit more strongly. When awake, he watched intently whatever was going on within his field of vision. He definitely knew his mommy and daddy, as he had from the beginning, and responded quickly to their touch and voices. Zach had been singing to him for hours: The Beatles, Led Zeppelin. Zach didn't know any traditional lullabies, but Caden didn't seem to care. He looked up intently at Zach as he sang, obviously enjoying Zach's choice of upbeat rock music. And whenever Zach stopped singing, Caden would start to fuss. He certainly responded to and loved the sound of his daddy's voice.

Lindsay commented that Caden actually seemed better than she had expected. She chuckled over his daily feeding of caffeine mixed into the breast milk, calling it "Caden's own little latte." Of course she was also very concerned, but her presence provided some distraction and a modicum of comfort for the rest of us. Her smiles were priceless, and her one liners made us laugh. Although her stay was too short, she was our best medicine and the breath of fresh air we had all needed.

On Thursday we dropped Lindsay off at the airport on our way back to Duke. I was beginning to worry about all the extra expenses of our daily trips to the hospital. After ten days we would get a break on our parking fees, but until then we were spending six dollars per car per day plus the cost of gasoline, which seemed to be always rising. Most days we still drove two cars. Zach wanted to be at the hospital early to talk to the doctors during their rounds and to check on how his boy had done since we had left the evening before. Although we were allowed and encouraged to call the hospital through the night as often as we wanted, it was still hard to have Caden out of our sight. Laurie, still recovering from her C-section, needed as much bed rest as possible; and she also needed to travel around her pumping schedule. Consequently, Zach often left at dawn to beat the rush hour traffic. Jay, Laurie, and I followed mid-morning.

Besides the cost of gas and parking, I quickly realized that lunch in the hospital cafeteria, no matter how reasonably priced, was still expensive for four adults; so I started packing our lunches to save money. Sometimes I would panic, thinking of the mounting medical expenses, but just as quickly I dismissed those concerns. In Scarlet O'Hara fashion, I would worry about that tomorrow.

The report Thursday morning was encouraging. Caden had had a good night. No suctioning had been required, and he had taken thirty milliliters of breast milk through a bottle, twice as much as the day before. The speech pathologist said his suck was getting stronger and more productive. The only medicine he was really getting was the caffeine to stimulate his breathing a bit. The surgeon had checked his thigh and found the incision healing nicely. Medically Caden was holding his own. We could all see some improvement. At least we thought we could. We were still waiting for test results.

Back in the nursery I sat with Laurie for a while keeping her company. She decided to do her "kangaroo care" with Caden, and the nurse helped her get settled in the recliner with Caden on her chest all warm and snug under a blanket. Before long both of them were again fast asleep. As I looked over at their sweet faces, my heart melted. Nothing was better than seeing my baby peacefully holding her baby.

In spite of all the stress, worries, and concerns, there were still many times when hope sang in my heart. Laughter followed tears. Dark moments faded. My emotions fluctuated from day to day, hour to hour, and sometimes minute by minute. A lot of sadness relentlessly weighed on my soul. Yet I refused to stay in a tunnel of despair. My family needed a strong mom and gramma. I was not about to let them down.

Chapter 9

"Shout for joy to the Lord, all the earth.
Serve the Lord with gladness; come before him with joyful songs.
Know the Lord is God. It is He who made us, and we are His."
Psalm 100:1-3

By Friday we had spent nearly two weeks mired in tension, fear, and uncertainty while sitting for hours on end in the NICU. Sleepless nights and mental overload had left us all drained and exhausted. I felt like I had run a marathon and couldn't imagine how Laurie was putting one foot in front of the other. She had not had any of the real rest which her body needed to recover from Caden's delivery. She was pumping her breast milk every three hours around the clock and making the daily ninety-mile round trip drive to Duke. I admired her resilience and courage. Only once had I really seen her break down and that was the week before when the doctor had given his grim prognosis. "I don't want to be one of those mothers whose baby dies," were the saddest words I had ever heard her say. I was worried about Caden; I was also worried about my daughter.

Although we arrived at Duke on Friday encouraged by Caden's slow, steady progress during the week, we still sat nervously awaiting the results of his muscle biopsy. Most of the day duplicated the previous few. Laurie rotated between Caden's bedside and the nursing room where she pumped her milk. Hoping to receive the test results soon, Zach lingered anxiously at Caden's bedside, waiting for the doctor. Jay and I set up camp in our self-assigned corner of the waiting area. When we grew tired of checking email or pacing restlessly, we took turns visiting with Caden or taking a break in the Ronald McDonald room.

More families like us arrived outside the nursery as the day wore on. Watching the newcomers appear, bewildered and overwhelmed, I sadly realized that after almost two weeks we were now the experienced NICU family members. I knew how to properly scrub my hands and don my gown. I knew where to get the free bottles of water and where to find the computers available for families to use. The bathrooms were down the hall by the elevators. The Ronald McDonald Room was over in the pediatric wing and required a pass from the receptionist in the NICU to verify a person's right to be there. Knowing the ropes, although convenient, was not a skill I appreciated having acquired and mastered.

During the afternoon, a clearly distraught woman I hadn't seen before came into the waiting room with a younger woman who had obviously just had a baby. Over time I learned that the new mom was actually a pediatrician herself at Duke. She had delivered a baby girl several weeks prematurely and now, accompanied by her own mother, had come to check on her child's condition. How hard, I thought, to be a pediatrician forced into the unfamiliar role of worried new mom. I felt sure she probably knew all there was to be concerned about, and I did not envy her professional knowledge.

Jay and I and the other grandmother quickly bonded over our shared circumstances. She celebrated with us as we told her of each little improvement Caden had made. In turn we tried to help her remain optimistic as, over the next few days, her granddaughter developed various preemie problems. Today that baby is healthy, but at the time the specialists' reports had us all worried.

That first afternoon when we met, Jay asked if we could pray with her, and she quickly agreed. Seated side by side in the waiting room, we joined hands and bowed our heads. Jay prayed aloud for strength and comfort and healing. Our faith continued to provide us with solace, and we were happy to share it.

Later in the afternoon, Zach and Laurie finally met with the geneticist and the head pediatrician of the NICU. Exactly one week earlier, they had delivered their heartbreaking prognosis for Caden. Would the results of the biopsy change anything? Jay and I sat and waited and prayed. When Laurie and Zach came to find us, one look at the expressions on their faces suggested the news had been encouraging. At last the doctors had an explanation for Caden's condition, and it wasn't what anyone had expected.

Caden, we learned, had been born with a rare genetic muscular disorder known as Congenital Fiber Type Disproportion or CFTD. We didn't fully comprehend it at the time, but we had just received the best diagnosis we could have hoped for. Caden had defied the odds and proven the doctors wrong. He was not suffering from a terminal condition. Of course he was far from out of the woods, as CFTD is a very serious disorder. The road ahead would be long and hard, but now we had something real on which to hang our hopes. Many other even more serious and often fatal conditions had been ruled out. We could now be cautiously optimistic about Caden's future. At the time it didn't occur to me how dramatically our expectations for Caden had changed in just two weeks. Instead of rejoicing at the birth of a healthy baby, we were now rejoicing that our baby would probably live.

We spent the rest of the day and evening trying to absorb the limited information the doctors could give us about CFTD and searching the internet for more. Caden's disease was extremely rare and incurable. The neurologist said it had been several years since he had seen his only other patient with the same disorder, a child who hadn't been diagnosed until he was older. The small number of known cases worldwide also encompassed a wide range of medical outcomes. We were hopeful that since the disease was not considered progressive and since Caden had already shown some improvement, his condition might be at the less severe end of the spectrum. The truth was that we would just have to wait and see. We had no idea what lay ahead, but we now felt Caden had a chance at living a full life. We were still blissfully unaware of all the challenges that would come.

Searching for more information than the doctors could provide, we found the following on the National Institute of Health web site:

Congenital fiber-type disproportion is a disorder that primarily affects skeletal muscles, which are muscles the body uses for movement. People with this disorder typically experience muscle weakness (myopathy) throughout the body, particularly in the muscles of the shoulders, upper arms, hips, and thighs. Weakness can also affect the muscles of the face and muscles that control eye movement (ophthalmoplegia), sometimes causing droopy eyelids (ptosis). Affected people may have joint deformities (contractures) and an abnormally curved lower back (lordosis) or a spine that curves to the side (scoliosis).

Approximately thirty percent of people with this disorder experience mild to severe breathing problems related to weakness of muscles needed for breathing. Some people who experience these breathing problems require extra support and use a detachable mask (noninvasive mechanical ventilation) to help them breathe at night, and occasionally during the day as well. About thirty percent of affected individuals have difficulty swallowing due to muscle weakness in the throat. Rarely, people with this condition have a weakened and enlarged heart muscle (dilated cardiomyopathy).

The severity of congenital fiber-type disproportion varies widely. It is estimated that up to twenty-five percent of affected individuals experience severe muscle weakness at birth and die in infancy or childhood. Others have only mild muscle weakness that becomes apparent in adulthood. Most often, the signs and symptoms of this condition appear by age one. The first signs of this condition are usually decreased muscle tone (hypotonia) and muscle weakness. Muscle weakness generally does not worsen over time, and in some cases it may improve.

Although motor skills such as standing and walking may be delayed, many affected children eventually learn to walk. These individuals often have less stamina than their peers, but they remain active. Rarely, people with this condition have a progressive decline in muscle strength over time. These individuals may lose the ability to walk and require wheelchair assistance.

(http://ghr.nlm.nih.gov/condition/congenital-fiber-type)

Although this information was far from totally reassuring, the Duke doctors guessed that Caden would do well. They felt sure he would eventually walk, even though they warned us that this and other physical milestones would surely be delayed. He would probably breathe without assistance. He would need lots of therapies, and he might require a feeding tube, at least for a while. In general they were optimistic that his life might be fairly normal. We understood that the future would probably present many challenges, but this was the best news we had received since Caden's medical journey began.

As Zach said, "I still have a baby in the NICU at Duke, but this is the best day since he was born."

We drove home that evening feeling as though a little of the tension had drained from our bodies. Suddenly we could breathe a bit more easily again. When I emailed the latest news to friends and family that night, I concluded, "God is good and powerful and has blessed this child and our family. He must have big plans for Caden."

Others were beginning to see what Zach had felt from the beginning: Caden most definitely was the perfect child for us. My friend Pam responded, "Woooo!!! Hoooo!!! This we can work with!... He is going to make it, and we will all cheer with every milestone. See what I mean about a soul choosing his parents? Who could better handle this little one than Laurie. She will be right there doing the physical therapy with the expertise only a mom could master." Then my son-in-law Rick's sister wrote, "They were meant to be Caden's parents." I smiled while reading these comments. Our little miracle baby already had his own cheering section!

Over the weekend we received another wonderful surprise to lift our spirits: a visit from Jay's brother Tom and his wife Margaret. They live in Southwestern Virginia and had driven over five hours to see us. Their totally unexpected arrival really brightened our day. Living in different parts of the country, we had not seen them for almost seven years. Knowing that they would drive so far to see their great nephew and offer us their moral support comforted us immensely. How wonderful to be a part of an extended family that comes when they're needed without even being asked.

Two weeks had now passed since Caden's birth. I felt like a totally different person. I left Maine expecting to come to North Carolina and spend three weeks enjoying my new grandson. I envisioned days spent rocking and cuddling and loving him. With the warmer Southern weather, I imagined Laurie and I would take him for walks in the stroller or on short outings in the car. I would help with the laundry, cleaning, and cooking while Laurie recuperated. We'd have this beautiful, loving family time together.

I had just helped my other daughter Lindsay and her family move and get settled into a rental while their new house was being built. It had been a lot of work. I was ready to relax. I couldn't wait to be a Gramma again. Jay looked forward to another grandchild as well. Laurie and Zach were excited to be parents for the first time and welcome their baby boy into the world after nine long months of waiting. We were all filled with such happy anticipation. This time was to be special and joyful and perfect. I was grateful for a diagnosis that was better than expected. I was thankful I could be with Laurie and Zach as they adjusted. I just couldn't help feeling we had all gotten cheated, and no one more than Caden.

Chapter 10

"Let the peace of Christ rule in your hearts, since as members of
one body you were called to peace.
And be thankful."
Colossians 3:15

Early Monday morning, exactly two weeks after arriving at Duke, Caden was moved from the NICU to the Transitional Nursery down the hall and around the corner. The Transitional Nursery consisted of a wide-open room which held about twenty-five babies. Instead of one nurse for every two babies, now there was one nurse for every four. The babies lay in cribs, not bassinets. Caden was at the end of a long row of cribs near the corner of the room. A mobile dangled over his bed to catch his attention, and the little blue musical monkey that Jay and I had bought for him shortly after his birth was tucked by his side. If we tried very hard and didn't think too much, we could almost fool ourselves into believing that our sweet baby was perfectly normal. The beeping monitor at his head, however, and the various leads still attached to his tiny body suggested otherwise.

About this time, because Caden's movements were so weak, he began retaining some fluid. My mind quickly imagined a couple of scary possibilities. What if he had kidney or heart problems? Due to Caden's rare and serious diagnosis, I had no trouble convincing myself that some additional malady waited in the wings. More tests were ordered for Caden, and fortunately all those came back with normal results. The nurse gave him a mild diuretic, and he gave her two soaked diapers. My mind temporarily rested a bit more easily.

Many of the same medical personnel who had cared for Caden in the NICU continued to monitor his progress in the Transitional Nursery. Although they were feeling more positive about his condition, I continued to fret. Waiting for Zach or Laurie to recount the doctors' reports after their daily morning rounds was nerve-racking. At first, if the day's evaluation of Caden sounded encouraging, I'd feel cautiously optimistic. Then all too soon my heart would grow heavy again as the many unknowns and what-ifs returned to haunt my thoughts.

Of immense comfort at those times was the sound of my mother's voice speaking softly inside my head: *Don't borrow trouble. Cross that bridge when you come to it. Take it one day at a time.* She had always taught me to stay positive, but this time I found her advice almost impossible to remember. Almost, but not quite. I found extra solace in wearing her wedding ring on a chain around my neck as I yearned for some tangible evidence of her spiritual presence. I really needed my mom, but her ring was as close as I could get.

At this point Caden's main challenge was to increase his oral feeds. Still too weak to nurse, he was able to drink about twenty-five percent of Laurie's breast milk by bottle; the remainder flowed through his NG tube. Whenever he took more milliliters by mouth, we all rejoiced. When he wore out sooner, our hearts sank.

On Tuesday of Caden's third week at Duke, Jay and I stayed back home in Clayton to do laundry and catch up on errands and household tasks. Although I had done little but sit in a hospital room for the past two weeks, I felt exhausted. The emotional stress was taking its toll on me, but I couldn't even begin to imagine how Laurie and Zach must be feeling. I worried about Laurie's mental health. After all, she had just gone through a nine-month pregnancy, a C-section, and the arrival of a baby with unexpected and serious medical challenges. The days she should have been relaxing, recuperating, and enjoying the new experiences of motherhood had never materialized. Instead, she and Zach made the long round trip to Duke where she spent endless hours alternating between sitting at Caden's bedside and sitting in the nursing room pumping her breast milk. The physical, mental, and emotional fatigue they felt must have been nearly unbearable.

Thankfully, friends, family, neighbors, our home churches, our social groups, and our workplaces all continued to help. For three weeks we came home to a hot meal delivered to our doorstep. Many friends sent money, gift cards, and gas cards. Notes and emails with sweet words of encouragement appeared daily. The occasional baby cards and baby gifts that Laurie and Zach received lent a sense of normalcy to Caden's arrival.

I knew some people were probably struggling with how to respond appropriately to his birth. With most newborns, the traditions are clearly in place. People send happy congratulatory cards, deliver cute baby gifts, bake cookies, or stop by for a visit with the new mom and baby. When that new baby is sick, the right card is hard to find. Questions abound. Is a toy an appropriate gift if Caden might never be able to play with it? What about an outfit with a sports motif if Caden ends up in a wheelchair? I'm sure people struggled with how to respond sensitively to Caden's birth. In fact, I know they did because one couple tried to stop the delivery of a pull toy that they had mailed before they knew of Caden's condition. Despite their efforts, the cute wooden-wheeled snail arrived anyway, and we loved it. True, he might never walk around pulling it, but then again maybe he would. I wish I could have told everyone personally how grateful we were for their thoughtfulness and how much we appreciated every act of kindness. That so many people reached out to help and comfort us in a myriad of ways meant so much and kept us going. Their thoughts, prayers, and concern wrapped us in a warm blanket of love.

On Wednesday Jay and I went back to Duke for the day. At 11 AM Caden was scheduled for a swallow study and an upper GI exam. Those tests involved an x-ray while he ate to see if he could swallow properly and protect his own airway. The doctors also wanted to make sure that the milk went down his esophagus correctly. If he was aspirating any milk into his lungs, he could quickly develop pneumonia or other breathing issues. When the time arrived for the tests, Laurie and Zach donned lead jackets and accompanied Caden and the doctors into the x-ray room.

Jay and I once again sat restlessly in the waiting room and tried not to fret. That particular day, Jay was more successful than I. Sometimes fearing the worst trumped any of my attempts to stay positive. Remembering all the people who were praying for us helped. At times, however, I felt like I was personally prayed out. I thought of the phrase so often repeated to us by friends and family: "I'm praying for you." Now I understood that people weren't just praying for Caden and the rest of us. They were praying in our place when the needed words failed us. What a blessing those prayers were. Still, I felt guilty that fears and doubts so often frequented my mind, creeping in like saboteurs to shake my faith. Jay reminded me that day that even the disciples were afraid as they sat through a storm in their boat. Very true, I thought, and this was quite a stormy ride we were having!

After another long wait, we eventually got the news that Caden had passed his swallow study. Another prayer answered. Another worry eased. Now Laurie and Zach could continue their attempts to bottle feed Caden with a little more confidence. Pam, my dear friend, responded to my email update that day with these words of love and encouragement: "This is absolutely fabulous news! . . . One of these days you are going to have to look in the mirror and realize you are a much stronger woman than you ever realized. Even soldiers shake! So march on my Lady, the troops are with you!"

Thursday and Friday brought a few more noticeable improvements. Best of all, Caden appeared to be a little stronger. While

Laurie held him upright with his head on her chest, for the first time he lifted his head slightly to try and look up at her. He continued learning how to suck, doing a little better each time with his bottle before finishing up with the necessary feeding using his NG tube.

More often than anyone liked, however, forceful vomiting followed his feedings. Once while I was holding him, formula suddenly spewed from Caden's nose and mouth all over us. The nurse quickly grabbed him out of my arms and began suctioning. Caden gagged and gasped for air. A weak, pitiful cry emerged amidst more suctioning and choking. Fortunately, that crisis, like many others, eventually passed, but it was horrifying to watch. My heart raced and pounded in my chest. The memories of feeding my own two daughters as babies, that quiet, peaceful, cuddling time, seemed very far removed from this current scene.

Therapy was also a big part of Caden's day. The physical therapist taught Laurie and Zach how to do some simple exercises with Caden's legs when he was awake. They pulled his knees up and together towards his chest and then circled them in a bicycle-pedaling motion. They also massaged the palms of his little hands and each tiny finger to stretch them. He tended to close his hands into fists with his thumbs tucked inside, and the doctors wanted to keep his hands flexible. Another exercise involved bringing his hands from his sides to the center of his mouth and back to his sides. The therapists were very encouraging, and Laurie's massage training certainly helped. Her abilities seemed like further evidence that God actually had already prepared her to be this special baby's mother.

As the days passed, we began to see God using Caden's medical issues for good. Caden had successfully stolen the hearts of all the doctors and nurses, and there were many who now knew of this special baby in the nursery. Doctors and nurses not even assigned to his case came by to see how he was doing. He had become quite the novelty. On Friday during rounds, one of the physicians remarked she had never seen a baby before with his condition. My guess was ninety-nine per cent of the medical staff at Duke had never seen a case of CFTD. At least it rendered Caden a lot of extra attention.

Jay and I spent as much time as possible taking turns sitting and holding our grandson. We knew the doctors were guardedly optimistic that he would live and thrive, but we also understood that many unknowns remained. No one could really tell us for sure what Caden's life would be like. Living with that uncertainty was already proving difficult. At first we were just happy that his diagnosis had not meant an immediate death sentence. As time passed, however, we began to realize that no one knew for sure the consequences of being diagnosed with CFTD. All those expectations that every new parent and grandparent has for their baby no longer applied to us. The hopes and aspirations we held for Caden before his birth now seemed perhaps to be just wishful thinking. The reality that remained was a very uncertain future.

When Jay and I weren't back in the nursery, we were usually out in the waiting room, still claiming the chairs in the corner by the drink machine as our own. Some of the same faces we saw when we had first arrived nearly three weeks before were still present. Others had been replaced with those of the newly-appearing moms and dads. The worried looks on everyone's faces were a shared expression.

One day as I sat there passing time, I noticed Marie, one of Caden's original nurses in the NICU, exit from the nursery with a tiny baby under her arm. Wrapped in a blanket and wearing a knit cap, the baby was practically hidden from view. There were no tubes, no monitors, no lines, and no equipment. Marie crossed the waiting room and entered another room through the door marked Family Room. At the time I wondered what to make of that. Why wasn't the baby in a bassinet? Why wasn't there any of the usual medical paraphernalia trailing along behind? I had never seen any nurse just walk out of the nursery simply holding a baby. Something looked very wrong; but before I had a chance to think about it much,

I was distracted by Laurie's appearance at my side. Only later would I fully understand the significance of what I had just seen.

After three weeks in North Carolina, the time arrived for Jay and me to say our goodbyes to our sweet grandson and his parents and return to our own home in Maine. We were leaving Raleigh the next morning for our long drive back. Zach's job allowed him up to twelve weeks of paid parental leave using his accumulated sick days. He and Laurie would be able to manage together. I planned to return to North Carolina when Caden was released from the hospital; however, we still had no idea how long it would be before that happened. We gave our grandson lots of cuddles and hugs and kisses before we left.

"Grow strong while we're gone," I whispered softly in his ear as I kissed him one last time before leaving the hospital. He had proven himself over and over again during the last three weeks to be "our little warrior," but the fight was far from over. We still really had no idea what would happen next.

Chapter 11

"And we know that in all things God works for the good of those who love Him, who have been called according to his purpose."
Romans 8:28

Daily over the next two weeks, Laurie and Zach continued their long drive back and forth between their home in Clayton and Duke University Children's Hospital in Durham. Caden slowly gained weight, and his respiration and oxygen levels stabilized. The monitors beside his crib alarmed much less frequently, and every day he seemed to grow a bit stronger. His feedings, however, remained a huge stumbling block to his being discharged. The doctors were encouraged by his increased ability to suck and swallow, but he could not consistently drink enough to sustain his growth without the ongoing use of the NG tube. He usually took some breast milk from a bottle several times a day; however, he tired quickly. So as not to waste his energy eating, he was offered a bottle first and then fed the remainder of Laurie's breast milk through his NG tube.

Some bottle feedings went better than others. At one session he might consume a half, three fourths, or even almost an entire feed by mouth. At other times he would barely swallow an ounce. When it didn't go well, Laurie experienced overwhelming feelings of frustration and failure. Obviously eating is a basic human activity, and feeding one's child is such a primal mothering instinct. To be unable to accomplish that simple task with ease and enjoyment broke Laurie's heart and mine too. I knew from experience what she was missing. That wonderful, close, nurturing experience of feeding her child was absent. Instead she was spending her time counting milliliters of milk and willing every drop down Caden's throat.

One day soon after Caden's arrival in the Transitional Nursery, a different pediatric attending, Dr. Stephany, came on duty for her two weeks of rotation. She began discussing the possibility of inserting a more permanent feeding tube into Caden's stomach. This procedure would allow for the removal of the NG tube, a less desirable long-term feeding method. Secure in knowing that his nutritional needs would be met, Laurie and Zach would finally be able to take Caden home. Dr. Stephany assured them that he probably wouldn't need the tube forever, but she insisted it was what was best for him now.

"Duke is good at saving babies. We aren't as good at growing babies. He needs to go home," she advised.

The downside to a feeding tube was that Caden would again have to undergo a surgery with all its accompanying dangers. Caden's condition and the particular gene involved put him at risk for what we now knew as anesthesia induced malignant hyperthermia, a rise in body temperature during surgery, which could be fatal. Various types of anesthesia and monitoring were discussed. After weighing the pros and cons, Laurie and Zach decided to follow the doctor's advice. With some apprehension, they requested that Caden be scheduled for surgery to insert a feeding tube.

In the meantime, in preparation for Caden's discharge after surgery, Laurie and Zach arranged to spend a night in the Family Room with him. They would totally care for Caden themselves, but the medical staff would be just steps away. The rooming-in got temporarily delayed, however, when another family had a greater need for the space. Sadly, their baby was dying, and they were going to spend their last hours together in the Family Room.

When Laurie told me this, I suddenly remembered the baby I had seen nurse Marie carry into that Family Room weeks earlier.

With heart wrenching clarity, I now understood why there had been no bassinet, no tubes, no monitors . . . just a dying baby in a nurse's arms. Suddenly a feeding tube seemed a minor bump in the road to keeping Caden nourished and alive. Laurie and Zach would be parents who got to take their baby home. They were two of the lucky ones.

Later that weekend Laurie and Zach had their rescheduled time alone with Caden just outside the security of the nursery, only footsteps away from any help they might need. According to Laurie, "Caden did great. Zach and I . . . not so much!" The uncertainties and attendant responsibility of taking home a medically fragile newborn became quickly apparent as the three of them settled in for the night. Having the full responsibility for Caden was nerve-racking, especially since he remained attached to his monitors, which sometimes beeped for no good reason except to scare his parents out of their intermittent sleep. Furthermore, Laurie was getting up to pump her breasts every three hours in addition to the time it took to actually feed Caden with first the bottle and then the tube.

At the time Caden was only averaging about fifty percent of any feed from the bottle alone. Once or twice a day he was allowed to sleep and just given one hundred percent of the breast milk through the tube. I thought at the time that many of us might find eating and sleeping simultaneously to be pretty convenient. For the adults, however, the process of feeding Caden seemed never-ending. He was fed every three hours, and it often took him thirty to forty-five minutes to eat. Laurie and Zach were permitted little time to sleep after the pumping, feeding, and diapering before the whole process began again. I know the morning after their night in the Family Room left them both wondering how they would ever manage Caden's care alone at home day after day.

Caden's abdominal surgery was scheduled for mid-morning on Wednesday. He was then one month and one day old. Unfortunately, 3 PM arrived before he went into the operating room, a very long day for Laurie and Zach to sit and wait at the bedside of an infant who hadn't been fed since midnight. Dr. Lin, the gastroenterologist, executed a perfect placement of Caden's G-PEG. That part of the procedure went well. However, since the insertion of the peg was more major than his earlier muscle biopsy, Caden had to be intubated this time. Fortunately, despite all the concerns, he came off the vent without any serious issues.

Because of the sedation, however, Caden had trouble remembering to breathe. This necessitated blowing air into his nose occasionally and giving him a little jolt of caffeine. The medicine used to reverse the effects of the anesthesia also reversed the effects of the pain medication. Caden was waking up and breathing, but he was also hurting. Sadly Laurie and Zach had the difficult task of watching their baby suffer. He was tiny and helpless, and he had already been through so much.

After a few hours in the recovery room, Caden eventually returned to the NICU for observation. A dose of morphine about midnight left him feeling more comfortable. By the next morning, he was bright-eyed and alert. Back in the Transitional Nursery, his respiration remained normal; and he began to take some breast milk. In my mind I could almost hear my mom's voice: *Things always look better in the morning.* Best of all, Caden was now a huge step closer to finally going home.

Chapter 12

"Ask and it will be given to you; seek and you will find."
Matthew 7:7

The plan had been for me to fly back to Raleigh when Caden was finally discharged from the hospital and to spend a couple of weeks helping to care for him. A mere two weeks after leaving North Carolina, I eagerly returned to welcome my grandson home.

Arriving on the weekend, I drove to Duke with Laurie and Zach on Sunday morning, anxious to see how Caden had improved in my absence. He still had a few monitors attached, but the nasal tube was gone. He now wore regular baby clothes and looked perfectly normal lying in his crib. Only the G-PEG on his belly under his sleeper belied his condition.

Before being discharged from Duke, Caden had to prove he could maintain his vital signs while sitting in his car seat for an hour and a half. Zach brought the seat into the nursery and placed it on the floor. For more than a month, it had remained empty and unused in the back seat of their car. Now the time had come to try it out.

Laurie picked Caden up out of the crib and settled him in place. He sat there fairly contented at first, but soon grew restless. Since it was late afternoon, he was obviously tired and hungry. Sitting patiently in his car seat for ninety minutes wasn't part of his plan. Soon he was crying hard with his rather weak voice as Laurie, Zach, and I watched helplessly. Frustrated, Zach went for a nurse and asked if this couldn't be tried again later after Caden had eaten.

73

The nurses agreed they would repeat the test after we had left for the day. I think they realized this car seat test might be better accomplished without the anxious observations of Mommy, Daddy, and Gramma. With that decided, Laurie comforted Caden and tucked him back into his bed. One last time we left the hospital without the baby and headed home.

A phone call to the nurses' station later that night assured us that Caden had passed his test and would be discharged the next day. For five long weeks we had eagerly awaited the words, *Caden is coming home*, and now we looked at each other with a mixture of joy and apprehension in our eyes.

The next morning, Monday, March 21, Laurie and Zach left for Duke bright and early to finally bring their baby boy home. I stayed behind to ready the house and give them some private family time. Hours later they arrived back in Clayton with Caden sleeping peacefully in his car seat. When I heard the garage door go up, I grabbed the camera and ran to greet them and document the long-awaited moment. Laurie was seated in the back next to the car seat, and Zach was driving. I could barely contain my excitement while they got Caden out of the car.

"Wait, let me get a picture," I cried.

There we all stood, each of us grinning from ear to ear. I had never seen that big of a smile on Laurie's face. Our little miracle baby was home at last. He was exactly five weeks old.

No longer having to make that long daily trip to Duke was such a relief. No one would miss the hours spent sitting restlessly in the waiting room. Though the absence of reassuring, knowledgeable medical personnel nearby felt scary, we were all so happy to have Caden home.

Caden's initial days out of the hospital went reasonably well. It was a delightful time of firsts: first time in his bouncy seat, first time in his swing, first tummy time on the living room floor, first bath, first walk in the stroller, first exercises. Laurie and Zach continued to work with Caden to increase the volume of his bottle feedings. Amounts varied from one feeding to the next, but whatever he didn't take from the bottle was poured through his GI tube directly into his stomach (a bolus feed). He'd now gained just about a pound since his birth over a month earlier.

A very contented baby, Caden only fussed when he got hungry or needed a diaper change. He definitely knew his mommy and daddy, those two special faces he saw leaning over his crib hour after hour for many weeks. He would fuss when they walked out of his sight and stop as soon as they returned. I proved an OK substitute in a pinch.

By the following week, Caden, then six weeks old, continued to do well. His days consisted mostly of eating, sleeping, and a little fussing. I'd already been showing him his books. As a former reading and English teacher, my reading to Caden would have surprised no one who knew me. I found he really liked the black and white pictures better than the colored ones. Guess the baby experts were right. Of course he also stared at the dark blades of the ceiling fan against the white ceiling. All about contrasts, I thought. I told him stories like "Goldilocks and the Three Bears," to which he listened intently, and "The Three Little Pigs," not so much.

Before long he started to coo in response to my talking, and he even gave us a few very tentative smiles. The doctors had assured us that Caden's mental development would be normal. It was wonderful to see those first reassuring signs.

Laurie and Zach also did physical exercises with him every day to increase his muscle strength. We could see that effort beginning to pay off. Learning to hold his head up was the hardest, and he definitely didn't like tummy time. As soon as we flipped him on his stomach, he would start to fuss and cry. His neck muscles were so weak he could only lie with his face pushed flat against the floor. We had to turn his head to the side for him to make sure he could breathe. When we held him on our laps facing us and sat him up, he struggled mightily to raise his head to look up at us.

Every night at 10 PM, Laurie or Zach hooked Caden up to an electric pump that stood beside his crib. The pump continuously fed him through his G-PEG, the tube into his stomach. At 6 AM Laurie would turn the pump off. Because Caden was struggling to get enough volume to support optimal growth, the pump provided him with continuous nutrition very slowly as he slept. It also provided him with very wet diapers, which sometimes disturbed his sleep. By the end of that first week, however, he was mostly sleeping through the night.

Unfortunately, the same couldn't be said for Laurie and Zach. Although the pump was feeding Caden, Laurie still got up every three hours to pump her breast milk. Since Caden was never going to be able to successfully nurse, Laurie decided the time had come to stop breast feeding. She was exhausted emotionally and physically, and her thyroid levels were all out of sync. She had been to the doctor herself for testing, and he was attempting to figure out a treatment plan for her. Laurie had given Caden the best start with breast milk that she could. Now the time had come for her to start taking care of herself. Caden needed good nourishment, but he also needed a healthy mommy.

Two weeks after Caden's arrival home, I flew back to Maine. Now Laurie and Zach had full responsibility for Caden, a very big job. Although all new first-time parents have some adjusting to do, fortunately most do not have babies with Caden's medical challenges and future uncertainties. How I wished I lived just next door or across town where I could be helpful on a daily basis. I know having me around was reassuring for Laurie, and I always tried to be as encouraging as possible. Never have I considered myself a true optimist; I worry a lot. Still, deep inside I believed this child would not only survive but live a good life no matter how long and hard the road ahead might be. I would try my best to convey that certainty to Laurie from a distance, but I knew she would miss my daily presence.

Nevertheless, I couldn't stay in North Carolina forever. I had a husband, another daughter, a son-in-law, and another grandchild waiting for me back in Maine. Reluctantly, I headed home. When granddaughter Cate finally saw me again after my return, she clung to me and whispered, "I missed you for a hundred hours." Laurie and Zach and Caden weren't the only ones who needed me. It felt good to be home.

Chapter 13

"He gives strength to the weary and
increases the power of the weak."
Isaiah 40:29

A few days after I flew home, Caden turned seven weeks old. On Tuesday, April 5, he returned to Duke for his first visit to one of the Special Infant Care Clinics. These monthly clinics were held for all the babies who had spent time in the NICU at Duke and had ongoing medical issues. Each baby was seen by a team of pediatric specialists who were a part of his or her continual monitoring and necessary care. In Caden's case that meant specialists in pediatrics, neurology, gastroenterology, speech therapy, physical therapy, urology, cardiology, and pulmonology.

Caden would be attending this clinic about every two months for routine examinations by a pediatric neonatologist and usually a checkup with speech and physical therapy. In addition, there would be periodic visits with each of the other individual specialists. Although these appointments required a long car trip and a full day spent consulting with specialists, Laurie and Zach found it oddly reassuring to be back at Duke. They knew that no matter what happened while they were at the hospital, medical personnel, some of the best in the country, were always nearby. They were also always eager to learn what kinds of gains and progress Caden had made since their last visit.

At this first appointment, the news was good. Caden had stayed healthy and was growing. He weighed eight pounds and three ounces, a gain of one pound and six ounces since birth. Though he was only gaining twenty-five grams a day compared to the ideal thirty grams, the doctors were still pleased.

Dr. Bentley, the pediatric neonatologist, gave Caden a full examination and addressed Laurie and Zach's general questions and concerns. She thought Caden's head control had improved and was happy to see him moving his head from side to side and also tracking properly with his eyes. His lungs and heart both sounded good, and his hips, legs, and ankles all appeared normal. Noting only that Caden's knees seemed a little stiff, she concluded her part of the exam and passed him along to Brooke, the physical therapist.

Brooke had worked with Caden since he had first arrived at Duke as a newborn. She attributed his stiff knees to tight hamstrings and showed Laurie how to stretch those tight muscles with massage. Again, with Laurie's own professional training in medical massage, she felt God's hand in providing her with the skills she needed to help her son. In this important way, Laurie was the perfect mom for Caden.

Brooke also showed her how to massage the scar on Caden's thigh. The chunk of muscle he was missing from his muscle biopsy made the surrounding skin pucker. Some massage should help smooth the area. Perhaps later, as an older boy, he would view the remnants of his wound as a "battle" scar to be proudly displayed to his future friends. Brooke also showed Laurie and Zach some other exercises that might strengthen Caden's core muscles.

As they neared the end of their physical therapy appointment, all the instructions began to sound like Gold's Gym for babies, but Brooke wasn't quite finished. She recommended thumb splints for Caden to wear three hours a day because he tended to keep his thumbs tucked inside his fists. When the day came for picking Cheerios up off the table, Caden would need nice flexible thumbs.

With a quick check of Caden's G-PEG by Dr. Lin, the pediatric gastroenterologist, Caden's two-hour exam ended. He would have weight checks and feeding adjustments at the local pediatrician's office every week or two and several appointments with some of the other pediatric specialists in the weeks to follow, but he would not be seen at Special Infant Care Clinic again for two months. Not until June.

When Laurie called that night with the medical update, Jay and I both felt relieved and reassured. Although many challenges lay ahead, for the moment we celebrated our miracle baby's good health. I tried to suppress any worries or doubts about what the future might hold and instead just relished the moment. I wish I could say I was one hundred percent successful. Each time we received an encouraging report, I immediately rejoiced with a prayer of thanksgiving; but that little nagging voice in the back of my mind questioning what the future might hold for Caden was never totally silenced.

At nine weeks Zach returned to his job at the crime lab, and Laurie assumed full responsibility for all of Caden's daytime care. This seemed like an awesome challenge for a first-time mom with a baby having special needs, but she rose to the occasion with a strength I admired. Caden's mental development progressed normally, and for that we felt very blessed. He smiled and cooed at the expected times. He responded to familiar faces and welcomed the appearance of neighbors and friends with happy recognition.

His physical limitations, however, already required some adjustments. His weaker arm muscles had us searching for toys and rattles that weren't too heavy. When I went to the store, I paid close attention to the recommended age range. If the package said newborn or 0-3 months, I considered buying the toy. Otherwise, I knew it would be too heavy for Caden. That wasn't so bad at first, when he was still just a few months old. I felt sadder six months later when I still had to choose his toys with similar care.

His feeding tube presented another set of unexpected challenges. Baby clothes with zippers down the front meant practically undressing Caden to feed him. For daytime I looked for outfits that snapped down the front. With those Laurie could just unsnap where his tube needed to be attached. At night when he was hooked up to his feeding pump for eight hours, the sleep sacks that zipped from the neck down to the bottom worked well. Laurie or Zach could just let the tubing come out at the bottom, which also prevented Caden from getting tangled up in it. Laurie often shook her head at the irony of safely removing the bumper pads, the blankets, and the stuffed animals from his crib and then putting him to bed with a long length of tubing.

The particular style of sleeper he needed also proved to be the most expensive in the stores. I began shopping local consignment shops and eBay to find better prices. Caden's expenses were quickly mounting and sending off baby clothes seemed like one way Jay and I could help; however, I felt guilty sending my new grandson gently-used baby clothes. I worried that Laurie would feel hurt with secondhand things, but I knew I could stretch my dollars so much further by steering clear of the department stores for certain items. Luckily she was always grateful; and, if she did mind, she never let it show.

The skyrocketing medical bills created a huge stress. Zach had decent family medical insurance through his job, but the premiums were high and still didn't begin to cover all their new expenses. During her pregnancy, Laurie and Zach had saved the money needed for deductibles and co-pays for a healthy baby. Now they were facing thousands of dollars in unexpected, out-of-pocket costs. Sometimes I couldn't help but feel angry at the unfairness of the situation. Because Caden was born sick instead of healthy, they had to meet a separate deductible for him. That meant an additional three thousand five hundred dollars above what they had already paid for Laurie and his actual birth. All of his doctors were specialists, which required a higher co-pay of sixty dollars per doctor's visit. His feeding pump, which cost six thousand dollars, and all his special feeding supplies were other unanticipated expenses. Even after deductibles, insurance covered only eighty percent of the cost until they met their yearly maximum. None of that included the cost of the frequent drives to Duke that weren't covered at all. Thousands of dollars of charges for which they were solely responsible began to mount up. Opening up the daily mail soon became an anxiety-producing task.

Over time the Explanation of Benefits forms sent by the insurance company grew to hundreds of pages. Trying to keep track of the hospital and doctor charges, insurance payments, and uncovered expenses they needed to pay out of their savings grew into a bookkeeping nightmare. Hours that Laurie couldn't spare while caring for a high-needs baby were spent making phone calls to doctors' offices and insurance companies and trying to keep accurate financial records. Setting up payment plans and worrying about paying bills in general began to take a toll on her mental health.

Laurie was unable to return to her job as a massage therapist as planned, so they struggled to get by on just Zach's salary. Jay and I constantly fretted over this aspect of their situation. If we could have paid for everything, we would have. The financial burden seemed so unfair on top of all the other worries and demands of a sick baby.

In the midst of all this financial strain, so many family members, friends, churches, and social groups continued to step up and help. Finding an appropriate card for a new baby or words to say to a family whose baby has medical issues can be difficult, yet the comforting and supportive messages poured in. Friends who sent baby clothes were so thoughtful to call and ask exactly what Caden needed. Should the sleepers close with zippers or snaps? What weight should the material be? Did he need long-sleeved or short-sleeved onesies? More gift cards for gas and groceries and other baby necessities like diapers and formula arrived. People sent cash to use as needed. Some of these people were not even close friends or family, but they had heard our story and responded with a wonderful sense of good will. We were overwhelmed by the outpouring of love and generosity. God was providing for us in ways in which we hadn't even known how to ask.

Now that Caden was a few months old, Laurie began the search for local physical and speech/feeding therapists, another unexpected expense but one they couldn't afford to ignore or postpone. On the advice of the Duke therapist, Laurie contacted the Infant and Early Childhood Program for their county. The services weren't free, but they would be charged on a sliding scale which left them to pay about forty percent of the cost.

First, a case manager arrived to do an evaluation of Caden's needs. Then the case manager contacted various local agencies to find therapists who would accept Laurie and Zach's insurance, who had time in their schedule for a new client, and who felt comfortable and skilled working with an infant having Caden's diagnosis. This whole process required many phone calls, meetings, paperwork, and approvals. Weeks passed before a physical therapist finally arrived to help Caden.

Nancy was a very knowledgeable, patient, and caring woman. Caden was not impressed. Therapy was hard work and uncomfortable. Watching as Caden fussed and cried and grew tired to the point of exhaustion was difficult for Laurie. Frequently he would become so upset, he would gag and throw up. There were many days when Laurie wished she could send Nancy on her way. It's hard to argue with success, however, and slowly Caden was making progress in tiny increments.

On May twenty-fourth, Laurie and Zach returned to Duke for a consultation with Dr. McDonald, the geneticist. They were there to receive the results of the genetic testing that had begun in February. Caden's tests confirmed his muscle biopsy. As Dr. McDonald explained, he had a mutation of the RYR1 gene on Chromosome 19. This mutation affects primarily the skeletal muscles and, in particular, the effect of calcium on muscle contractions. Laurie and Zach had previously had their own bloodwork done, and Dr. McDonald now had those results too. Apparently Zach shared the same three mutations on the third, fourth, and fourteenth exon (an exon is a section of a gene) that Caden had. Zach, however, had no signs or symptoms of CFTD himself. Furthermore, Laurie had no mutations at all on that gene. Having checked for mutations, the lab would now begin looking for insertions and deletions to explain Caden's condition. More bloodwork was ordered. More extensive testing was required. More time to wait.

Laurie and Zach were urged to contact the Beggs Laboratory in Boston, Massachusetts. Affiliated with Boston Children's Hospital, that facility does research on various neuromuscular disorders including the causes of CFTD. Dr. McDonald also reiterated that currently there is no cure and that much is still unknown about this rare condition.

"Time will tell," was the doctor's prognosis.

Unfortunately, the meeting with the geneticist had left them with more questions than answers about Caden's condition.

Later that same day they met with Dr. Smith, a pediatric neurologist and a muscle specialist. He had examined Caden his first few days in the Duke NICU. Zach and Laurie immediately liked him and his upbeat, positive attitude. He reconfirmed Caden's physical challenges but also gave them practical and encouraging advice. He recommended that a cardiologist and pulmonologist check and monitor Caden regularly just to be on the safe side. CFTD does not normally affect the heart, but respiratory problems can occur because of the weaker chest muscles. He kindly acknowledged their financial concerns and put them in touch with a social worker who might be able to help them find some assistance. He even gave them his phone number so they could call with any questions and hopefully eliminate the need for another office visit and co-pay for at least the next six months. Most encouraging of all, he told them to try not to worry about where Caden was and where he should be with regards to his physical development.

"Nobody can tell you for sure what he will or won't be able to do," Dr. Smith explained. "Let Caden be Caden."

Caden was definitely providing an important life lesson for our family about living in the moment and living with a grateful heart. Many prayers had already been answered as many more were being requested. I sometimes felt like God must surely be tired of hearing my voice. Nevertheless, I believed now more than ever that God had put Caden here on earth and here with our particular family for a reason. God had special plans for him, and He was giving us the privilege of witnessing those plans unfold.

"Let Caden be Caden," God whispered in my heart. "Let me do My work and trust in Me completely."

Chapter 14

"Therefore go and make disciples of all nations, baptizing them in the name of the Father and of the Son and of the Holy Spirit . . . "
Matthew 28:19

Jay and I returned to North Carolina for a week-long visit in the middle of June. On Sunday, June 19, which was Father's Day, we witnessed Caden's baptism at the Greater Heights Methodist Church in Clayton. Jay and I bought him a cross necklace which he wore during the church service that day. Laurie baked a cake for celebrating afterward and decorated it with Caden's name and the outline of a cross. Joy filled our hearts. Only a few months earlier we had not known if this day would ever be possible.

We arrived at the service in anxious anticipation. With Caden nestled in his father's arms, Zach and Laurie walked up on the stage of the theater the church used for its services. Pastor Matt, dressed casually in sandals, torn jeans, and an oxford shirt with the sleeves rolled up, stood waiting for them. As Zach held Caden, Pastor Matt began to utter the holy words of baptism and prayer. Caden stared intently into his eyes. The whole congregation watched from their seats, rejoicing in the life of this special baby. My eyes filled with tears as I looked on. I've always loved the part of the baptismal service where the pastor makes the sign of the cross on the baby's forehead and calls him "child of God." Caden was surely God's own: loved, protected, and cherished. In God's eyes every one of us has special needs. In God's eyes Caden already was His perfect creation.

Caden, now four months old, weighed eleven pounds and eight ounces. Although he was only in the fifth percentile in weight, he continued to grow and stay healthy. He was a very happy, contented baby, who melted everyone's heart with his smiles. The only time he fussed was when he needed his diaper changed or when he threw up after a feeding. Unfortunately, his vomiting continued on a daily basis; the cause was yet to be determined.

His next scheduled visit to Duke's Special Infant Care Clinic was June twenty-first. Laurie and Zach left home by seven in the morning in order to arrive at the hospital and be ready for Caden's first appointment at eight-thirty. Over the following six hours, he was examined by Dr. Malcolm, one of the many neonatologists who had seen Caden in the NICU; Amanda, the speech therapist; Brooke, the physical therapist; Dr. Wechsler, the cardiologist; and Dr. McDonald, the geneticist. Everyone commented on how sweet and happy Caden remained over the course of a long day of poking and prodding. As the cardiac nurse said, "Even when I was putting those electrodes on his chest, he just looked up at me and smiled." The tests confirmed that Caden's heart was functioning perfectly. He wouldn't need to be checked again for another year.

Thanks to Laurie and Zach's consistent, hard work, the physical and speech therapists were also pleased with Caden's progress. Their support and encouragement were always appreciated.

Later, the neonatologist spoke with them about his feeding issues. Because a lot of what went down came back up, he recommended slower feeds and slower increases in volume. Since Caden continued to eat every three hours, feeding already took up a large portion of his day. Although Laurie had stopped pumping and had put Caden totally on formula, that change did not greatly simplify his feeding regimen. Every morning she or Zach mixed Caden's powdered formula very precisely in ever-changing proportions both to account for his growth and to enrich it with extra calories. Just correctly preparing it for the day was a time consuming and mathematical challenge. Following the doctor's suggestion to further slow the flow of his eating would necessitate spending even more time actually feeding him. That would leave even fewer hours in the day for therapy, sleep, and normal baby activities. While eating, Caden sat in a special feeding chair, was tube fed by gravity, and remained seated for fifteen to twenty minutes afterward in the hopes that he wouldn't throw it all back up. Sadly, the typical peaceful, cuddling time that feeding a baby usually provides was nearly absent. For Laurie, meal time with Caden was mostly work and worry.

On the bright side, Caden's mental development continued on schedule; and we counted our blessings. He smiled, cooed, and played with his toys while lying on the floor or sitting propped in his bouncy seat. He had learned to roll to his left side, and once or twice he had even made it over to his tummy. He still couldn't lift his head up while lying on his stomach, however, or push himself up at all on his arms. When he did make it over from his back to his tummy, he could only lie face down and squall in frustration. We rejoiced at his achievements and tried not to focus on the challenges.

I had been researching CFTD and genetic testing and soon came to realize how very complicated it all was. I was learning a lot although I still had only a rudimentary knowledge of a very complex subject. I googled and searched and read and questioned. I bookmarked web sites and talked to friends and family who had scientific or medical training. Somehow knowledge felt like control. If I could just understand what was wrong with Caden, maybe I'd find his condition less frightening. Maybe hope was out there. Maybe someone somewhere was finding answers. Maybe someone would eventually find the cure. Maybe sometime, but not yet.

Early on I discovered and joined a Facebook group comprised of individuals living with CFTD. Many of those affected were just babies and young children, so their family members, searching for information and help, also belonged. This group provided a great means of connecting with other moms and dads and grandparents sharing similar experiences. There were participants in Australia, Canada, Sweden, and other spots around the world as well as in many different states in the US. I was surprised at how small the group was. When I first joined, less than fifty individuals of various ages with Caden's diagnosis were represented. Caden was the youngest member at the time, but there were other preschoolers, young children, teenagers, and adults.

Most families had only one child affected, but in one situation a mom and her two daughters, who were both in their twenties, were all three diagnosed with CFTD. About a year after I joined, the older daughter died. She was only twenty-four, and everyone in the group was deeply affected by her death. My heart nearly stopped at the news. We shared the mother's grief from a distance and offered our sympathy in our online comments. We silently prayed we would never have to walk in her footsteps.

Although the CFTD sufferers shared many similarities in their conditions, they also exhibited a wide range of outcomes. Some were in wheelchairs, had tracheotomies, or were totally vent dependent. Some, like Caden, were tube fed. Some choked easily. Others ate normally. All had some muscular difficulties of varying degrees: going up steps, climbing, lifting, getting up from the floor. Many were susceptible to respiratory infections requiring lengthy hospitalizations. Many had endured leg braces, spinal fusions, and other joint difficulties. A few had heart complications. Some stayed relatively healthy. Most were very thin. All had poor muscle tone and reduced energy and stamina for physical activities.

This group provided Laurie and me with knowledge and support. Who better to ask our myriad of questions than others who had already been through it. What's the best type of feeding pump? How do you alleviate the formula-induced constipation? What type of orthotics do you use? With the combined experience of many families, someone always seemed to have a better answer than the doctors or specialists. Since so little was known about CFTD, experience seemed to be the best teacher.

Sometimes the shared information was scary. Would this or that complication eventually affect Caden? Someone else's crisis was a cause for a particular worry we hadn't even considered before. More often than I cared to admit, I thanked God, with a bit of guilt, that that particular problem was not on our plate, at least not now and hopefully never. The support, prayers, advice, and, yes, love that we all shared as a group were treasured. We were a community of survivors of a muscular disorder that challenged us all in many different ways.

We were present for each other . . . always. We encouraged Myra, whose daughter Letty is on a ventilator. Having lost the services of her night nurse, Myra was sometimes "on duty" for sixty-two hours straight. We prayed for Marissa, who had chronic Lyme disease and multiple heart issues herself. She was the primary caregiver for Rohan, a four-year-old who, despite his CFTD, was a pretty active little boy with many needs. We rejoiced with Fiona, whose six-year-old Flynn adjusted well to school in spite of his limitations. And we rallied around Sammy, whose mom Jeanette began raising money for CFTD research. I sent a donation and bought T-shirts. These children and parents and grandparents became my heroes. If they could cope with the challenges of CFTD, so could Jay and I, so could Laurie and Zach, and so would Caden.

Chapter 15

"The Lord is my shepherd, I shall lack nothing.
He makes me lie down in green pastures, he leads me beside quiet
waters, he restores my soul."
Psalm 23:1

Over the Fourth of July, Scott and Sarah, Laurie and Zach's next-door neighbors, invited them to the beach for a few free days of vacation. This would be their first overnight trip with Caden, and they immediately had some misgivings about going. What if Caden cried the whole way in the car? What if he wouldn't sleep at the beach house? What if they forgot some needed equipment? What if he got sick? Every parent knows the challenges that traveling with a baby present, but Caden's condition created some unique concerns. With lots of encouragement from friends and family, however, they decided to go; and they had a great couple of days. What a treat to be able to spend a little time as close to normal as possible: going to the beach, hanging out with friends, laughing and having fun. Bringing all the extra paraphernalia along that Caden required was a bit of a hassle but well worth the trouble.

I loved seeing the pictures of Caden dressed in his little swim trunks, sitting in Laurie's lap on the porch of the beach house. The smile on Laurie's face as she gazed down at him warmed my heart. This normal interaction between a mom and her baby was so rare for them. For a minute I could just admire Caden's photo and imagine there wasn't anything wrong with him. Nothing to worry about. A perfect illusion captured by the camera.

Caden's condition was definitely teaching me to appreciate the simple things. Although it was sometimes nearly impossible not to fear what tomorrow might bring, I knew I would have to learn to live with a great deal of uncertainty. Every time Laurie called to tell me about something new Caden had accomplished, my eyes filled with tears of joy. What he might never be able to do was the unspoken question, but I refused to let that thought strip me of my joy. I was successful about half of the time.

Soon after that brief vacation, Caden turned five months old. His most recent physical achievement had been learning to turn his head from side to side while lying on his tummy. He definitely preferred this to having his face flat against the floor. He could also now roll to both his left and right sides. He was still trying to push himself up on his arms while lifting his head, but he just wasn't strong enough yet. That didn't stop him from trying, however, and fussing in frustration when he failed. Laurie and Zach continued to do exercises with him each day to improve his strength and encourage equal muscle development on both sides of his body.

As of July first, the company providing Nancy, Caden's in-home physical therapist, had raised its co-pay due to budget cuts. Unable to afford the extra two hundred dollars a month in out-of-pocket costs, Laurie and Zach reluctantly put the therapist's services on hold and began working more with Caden themselves. The physical therapist at Duke, sympathetic to their circumstances, was quick to provide Laurie with plenty of direction on what to do. With her massage therapy background, Laurie was able to skillfully take up the challenge. Since the local physical therapist had only been coming for an hour a week and since Laurie worked with Caden daily, his progress continued unabated. To Caden, therapy was play. He laughed, giggled, and loved all the attention. Cooing had now escalated to shrieking, another good sign of his improving lung strength.

Feeding, as always, remained extremely challenging. By then he was resisting most bottles as though he had decided sucking was just too much work. More and more he relied on just the tube feeding, and both Laurie and Zach were frustrated. When Caden left the NICU, the doctors thought he would be bottle-fed in a matter of weeks. As weeks turned into months, the situation grew discouraging. His regimented three-hour feeding schedule during the day left Laurie little time for anything else. By the time she was done feeding Caden, he was ready for a nap. When he awoke, the feeding resumed. After squeezing in some additional time for therapy, Laurie had few precious moments left for just enjoying Caden. With no end of this routine in sight, adjusting to a new normal so different from what they had anticipated when Laurie was pregnant became their greatest challenge.

About then Laurie started back to work part time. She had found a new job as a massage therapist at The Club at Flowers Plantation, the recreation center in their planned community. Located about five minutes from their house, the facility had indoor and outdoor pools, tennis courts, workout rooms, and spa services. She was able to work two evenings a week and Saturdays while Zach was home with Caden. The job also included a family membership to the club, which was a nice benefit.

Although working cut into what little couple time she and Zach shared, Laurie appreciated the opportunity to make some money to help with the mounting medical bills. She also enjoyed spending a few hours away from the house with some adult company. Knowing Caden was being well cared for by his daddy while she was at work gave her peace of mind. Having the energy to work after caring for Caden all day, however, was a challenge. Her days were full and exhausting, and her sleep was often interrupted. Zach left for work before dawn each day, and he too returned home tired. I don't know how he managed to get up so early after being up and down all night with Caden as well. Regardless, she and Zach did all that needed to be done every day without complaint.

Chapter 16

"Trust in the Lord forever, for the Lord, the Lord,
is the Rock eternal.
Isaiah 26:4

By August I was more than ready for a return trip to North Carolina. Jay was between jobs and was free to accompany me, so we eagerly made our plane reservations. I couldn't wait to see the changes in Caden that the last two months had brought. Babies grow and change so quickly. I knew I had missed a lot in those weeks since we had last visited. With all the challenges Laurie and Zach faced, I hoped our arrival would also provide good moral support and practical help.

At six months Caden weighed fourteen pounds and four ounces. He remained in the fifth percentile on the weight charts, but at least he was growing at his own pace. His recent checkup at Duke had brought lots of encouraging news. Laurie and Zach had seen Amanda, the speech therapist, for a feeding evaluation. She felt that Caden was still experiencing a lot of reflux, which could be making swallowing painful for him. Perhaps this explained his frequent refusal to even try the bottle. She consulted with one of the pediatric neonatologists who had seen Caden in the NICU. Together they decided to try treating him with Prilosec, an even stronger medicine for reflux than the antacid he had been taking. At times like this we felt that no one really had any certain answers for Caden's difficulties. Often the doctors just seemed to be experimenting with our baby. At the very least, treatment was often a matter of trial and error. Nevertheless, with so little known about his condition, what else were they really supposed to do? Any guaranteed solutions to Caden's problems or definitive answers to our questions were obviously wishful thinking on our parts.

Just to complicate matters, Prilosec doesn't come in a liquid form, so transitioning Caden to that medicine required finding a compounding pharmacy. With Caden nothing ever seemed easy. Maintaining some semblance of patience and optimism always proved challenging, and it was hard to distinguish between the big problems worth fretting over and the smaller problems that were irritating but weren't cause for as much concern or wasted emotional energy. Fortunately, God ignored our craziness and continued to answer the prayers we didn't even know how to pray. Laurie eventually found that the local pharmacy in Clayton could fill the prescription. After several additional calls to the insurance company and the pediatrician, the prescription issues got resolved. Unfortunately the compounded medicine was more expensive, another necessary drain on the family budget, and we had no idea if it would even help Caden. We could only hope it would be worth a try.

While at Duke that day, Laurie and Zach had some time to spend between appointments, so they took Caden back to the NICU for a visit. When their names were announced over the intercom system, some of the doctors and nurses who were available came out to the waiting room to see one of their former miracle babies. Marie, one of our favorite nurses, actually cried when she saw Caden. She was the nurse who had prayed with us the day we were told he might die. Seeing him not just alive but thriving completely overwhelmed her.

"This completely made my day," she said with a broad smile.

Later that same afternoon, they had another appointment with a different specialist. Since it takes muscles to breathe, Caden's pediatric neurologist wanted a consult with a pediatric pulmonologist to see how, if at all, the CFTD was affecting Caden's breathing. First, they tested Caden's oxygen levels, which were good. Then the nurse put a mask over his face and tested him with a nebulizer to see if he needed that type of assistance. No problem there. Finally, she held a mask over his face and tested his lung strength. Laurie said the nurse described the procedure as trying to breathe through a tiny straw. This measured how much strength Caden had to breathe in and out. It's difficult to get an accurate reading on a baby that young so his score of forty, far below the normal eighty to one hundred, was hard to interpret. Other observable signs that he was breathing well such as his color and his oxygen levels, however, were acceptable.

As Caden started squealing at the top of his lungs, the doctor smiled and said, "See, that's what I mean. It takes lung strength to make that much noise."

Caden had come so far from those pitiful, weak mewling sounds he had made as a newborn. No breathing interventions or further lung testing would be required for now, just close monitoring and a recheck in four months.

Despite all that good news, the visits to Duke remained emotionally stressful, and they also contributed to Laurie and Zach's financial worries. Each appointment with a specialist required a co-pay, and Caden usually saw several specialists at each visit. The price of gas and lunch added up. In this instance, they also had another prescription to fill, the pricey compounded Prilosec. A single trip to Duke could easily cost them several hundred dollars beyond what insurance covered. Together they made too much money to qualify for assistance and not enough to pay the mounting bills without hardship. How were they going to manage this month after month? "God will provide" was sometimes little comfort. I tried not to worry about their financial concerns, but many nights I lay awake wondering how they were going to manage.

Chapter 17

"Fear of man will prove to be a snare,
but whoever trusts in the Lord is kept safe."
Proverbs 29:25

Back in June, Laurie and Zach had heard about a program which would provide them with some financial help with Caden's medical expenses, if he qualified. While tube feeding Caden at church one Sunday, a church member, who happened to be a nurse, approached them and asked if they were a part of the CAP-C program. Based on the child's condition rather than the parents' finances, this Medicaid waiver program in North Carolina was meant to help middle-income families like theirs with big medical expenses. She felt Caden would qualify because of his feeding tube. Laurie and Zach checked it out, felt they qualified, and completed the required paperwork. The approval process and consequent waiting list, however, were long. Until Caden made his way to the top of the list and was officially accepted for financial assistance, they were still on their own.

With no other option, Laurie and Zach continued to do Caden's physical therapy themselves, using the advice and suggestions from Duke. Because Caden had received some services before the co-pay got too expensive, he was listed in the case manager's files as temporarily inactive. As a result, she still came every six to eight weeks for a home visit to update Caden's health information.

In August she arrived right on schedule with pen and check-list in hand. Basically a pleasant, friendly woman, she made herself comfortable on one end of the couch while Laurie sat at the other. I was on the floor with Caden trying to keep him entertained while the two of them talked. It was hard not to feel a bit intimidated as she began her set series of questions. Can he sit up? Can he roll over? Can he do this? Can he do that? The reality was he was meeting many of his milestones but was definitely delayed in the area of gross motor skills.

As Laurie quietly and conscientiously responded to each question, I could tell she was hoping her answers might indicate that Caden was now in the normal range of development. It was hard not to hope that all the experts had been wrong and what first appeared to be a serious condition was now just a little minor delay. In our eyes he had been making huge strides, but what would the expert's assessment be? Every time Laurie answered a question with "No," I could hear the anxiety in her voice.

Finally reaching the end of her checklist, the case manager looked up from her paperwork and said, "Caden's doing so well. Think how much he'd be doing if he'd been receiving regular ther-apy."

An angry retort rose in my throat, but I bit my tongue and let Laurie answer for herself.

"That," said Laurie, "is because his daddy and I work with him every day, not just an hour a week like a physical therapist would do."

Flustered, the case manager quickly recanted her prior judg-ment. Most parents, she said, were not that diligent in working with their babies.

Although I was very sorry that Laurie had been subjected to the inappropriate comments of an ill-informed professional, my heart swelled with pride at her ability to handle the situation. My little girl was becoming a stronger, more capable woman every day.

She knew how to stand up for herself, and she would soon learn how to advocate for Caden.

My opinion of this case manager was less than glowing. Such a thoughtless comment for a healthcare provider to make, I thought. Certainly Laurie and Zach felt guilty that they couldn't provide Caden with the recommended therapies, but they were doing a great job themselves. Little did the case manager know that Laurie and Zach spent hours every week working with Caden and that his progress was largely the result of their dedication. More undeserved guilt poured on a wonderful mom and dad who were very successfully doing the best they could broke my heart.

While Jay and I were in Clayton, we tried to help out in every way possible. We brought some new clothes for Caden, and we bought diapers, formula, and groceries. We picked up some new toys and anything for the house we thought they needed. Our efforts were small but greatly appreciated. What we really wanted was to buy Caden a healthy body. Since that was beyond our power, we did what little else we could.

By then Caden had decided tummy time was not so bad after all now that he could move his head back and forth and lift it up briefly while on his belly. He was beginning to sit up pretty well while supported and could hold his head up off our shoulders when held. His mental and social development seemed normal. He laughed, giggled, shrieked, and "talked," maybe not with as much gusto as another six-month-old but a long way from those early weak cries at birth. The way he picked up his toys and threw them on the floor was also reassuring that his fine motor skills were developing on track.

My feelings at this point were conflicted. I no longer felt Caden's life was in imminent danger. My heart soared to see all his growth and physical accomplishments. However, did I ever feel angry or sad? Yes. Did I struggle with the despair that Caden had been born with a serious condition? Of course. Did my heart still break for the lost dreams and expectations we had all held for this precious baby before he was born? Absolutely. I wanted to just relax and enjoy Caden like I had my other grandchild. I wanted a new baby in the family to be fun, not hard.

Truthfully, I felt very guilty and selfish for thinking those things. I really just wanted Laurie and Zach to be able to relax and enjoy parenting without all the extra worry and stress. I wanted their baby to be doing all the things other six-month-old babies could do. I wanted normalcy. To ease my concerns, a friend reminded me that normal is "just a setting on the washing machine."

Slowly I began to focus on the reality that our family had received this beautiful baby boy who melted our hearts. We had a grandchild with an uncertain future, but really, everyone's future is uncertain. We had a grandchild with limitations, but isn't that true of us all? Who doesn't have some sort of disability or special needs? Those labels could be applied to anyone, and I knew we must not let them define Caden. I had a grandchild who was teaching me the lessons of patience, acceptance, gratitude, and faith. A six-month-old was making me into a better human being. I had the perfect grandchild for me.

As always, the most frustrating part of Caden's daily life continued to be his feeding. Caden was refusing to take anything at all from the bottle now, and almost daily he threw up after one or more of his tube feedings. This was not just a little spitting up. This was formula simultaneously pouring out his nose and mouth. That usually prompted a choking, coughing, gasping episode which required Laurie or Zach to immediately suction him. They did this with a little green bulb syringe given to all new parents at the hospital, and it clearly was not very effective for Caden.

One evening while we were visiting, Caden vomited and then choked. Jay and I were terrified. It took every ounce of my self-control to remain calm as Caden screamed and gasped. His crying just caused more mucous in his nose and throat which led to more gagging, more suctioning, more crying. A vicious cycle ensued. Laurie and Zach also began to look frantic as the episode continued.

Caden seemed unable to catch his breath. I actually thought we might need to call 911.

In desperation, I asked Laurie if I could try to calm him. I took Caden and put him up on my shoulder. Slowly I walked from room to room patting him on the back and talking soothingly. After about fifteen minutes, Caden improved; but an hour or more passed before Caden was calmed, changed, and back asleep. By then we were all exhausted physically and emotionally. I found it hard to imagine how Laurie and Zach were dealing with this on a daily basis, day after day, week after week. Somehow they managed, and I felt so proud of them both. Their lives were not easy, and there were many scary moments when Caden's life seemed very vulnerable and fragile.

Chapter 18

"Trust in the Lord with all your heart
and lean not on your own understanding."
Isaiah 26:4

In September Caden turned seven months old. The time for another visit to the Duke Special Infant Care Clinic had arrived. These scheduled appointments every two months provided a means for the doctors to keep tabs on Caden's development. Laurie called that night to fill us in on the results of his most recent check-up.

Dr. Malcolm and Dr. Bentley, the neonatologists, were very pleased with Caden's progress. They saw a healthy, happy baby who had made lots of progress physically and, his CFTD aside, appeared perfectly normal in every other way. He now weighed fifteen pounds and four ounces, still claiming the fifth percentile as his own. At twenty-six and three quarters inches in length, he was in the fiftieth percentile in height. They were glad his weight was on the chart and only concerned that it should remain there. He was obviously going to be tall and thin, just like his daddy.

After checking him over, Dr. Bentley said, "We all remember Caden, and we are amazed at his progress from when we first saw him as a newborn." Laurie and Zach looked at each other and breathed a sigh of relief. Those reassuring words meant so much.

Caden also had scheduled appointments with the Duke speech and physical therapists. Brooke, the physical therapist who had treated Caden in the NICU, was ecstatic with his improvements.

"He's physically delayed but not a ton." As she and Laurie practically jumped for joy, Brooke's student assistant looked on rather puzzled.

In response to her bewilderment, Brooke declared, "You just don't understand what this baby's been through and the progress he's made." But Brooke knew, and she was thrilled at how well Caden was doing.

The next stop was the gastroenterologist's office. The feeding issues still had everyone, including the specialist, looking for answers. First, he weight-adjusted Caden's Prilosec and prescribed a different, more gentle formula. Believing that the frequent vomiting was probably due in part to the tube feeding itself or to weaker muscles in the digestive tract, the doctor felt that as Caden got older and stronger he would outgrow this difficulty. He also thought that as Caden eventually transitioned to solid foods, his feeding issues would subside.

The truth of the matter was, the doctor really didn't know. He had never treated a CFTD baby before. They discussed the possibility of checking out his tummy with another endoscopy but tabled that idea for the time being. The procedure would require another anesthetic, which they all wanted to avoid. Two drugs that might help Caden's digestion had risky side effects so a "no go" there also. Another suggestion was to feed him more slowly a time or two a day with the pump rather than the bolus. Unfortunately that would even further limit his time for napping, playing, therapy, etc. No acceptable alternatives were really offered. For the time being, it looked like keeping plenty of extra clothing handy for changes and the bathtub nearby for clean-ups were the only available options. The doctors were happy as long as Caden was growing and healthy. Vomiting didn't concern them much. We could only pray that God and time would continue to heal.

The last meeting of their very long day at Duke was with the pediatric urologist. In November Caden was scheduled to have some minor urological surgery to correct a common condition unrelated to his other issues. For most babies the operation would be relatively simple. Since anesthesia was involved, however, no procedure on Caden could be labeled minor. On the other hand, November was two months away, so at least the concerns could be postponed until later.

Caden had done well all day without his regular naps and with lots of strangers poking and prodding. He had catnapped in his stroller and handled the appointments good naturedly with smiles and coos for everyone. Another full day of medical check-ups was finally over. The long ride back to Clayton was all that separated them from home and the end of an exhausting day.

The rest of September flew by uneventfully. Laurie continued working with Caden to develop his muscle strength. CFTD was not considered progressive, and since no one could really say what his muscle potential would ultimately be, Laurie and Zach hoped for the best. He had definitely gotten stronger since birth. His best chance for an optimal outcome seemed to reside in his therapy. They continued to wait for CAP-C approval, and, in the meantime, Laurie continued to work with him herself. She called me with daily updates, and one day I could hear the frustration in her voice.

"I just wish I could play with Caden without having to consider if this was something that would help him get stronger," she said sadly. "Some days I feel like all I do is clean up puke and exercise his muscles."

Tears welled in my eyes. She only wanted what every mommy wants: a typically developing, healthy baby. How often had we all heard or said the words: "I don't care what I'm having as long as he/she is healthy"? Spoken so often with careless ease, those words now rang hollow. Nothing I could say or do would change what Laurie and Zach and Caden lived with every day. My heart ached for her, but I couldn't fix it.

Chapter 19

*"So do not fear, for I am with you; do not be dismayed for I am
your God. I will strengthen you and help you;
I will uphold you with my righteous right hand."*
Isaiah 41:10

In early October I flew back to North Carolina to help Laurie
with Caden while Zach was in Washington, DC, at a work conference. Caden was now almost eight months old. He was finally sitting
up unsupported for short periods of time. He enjoyed playing with
his stacking rings and knocking over wooden blocks. His fine motor
skills seemed age appropriate, which I found very reassuring. I noticed myself constantly searching for evidence that Caden was a normal baby, although I always felt guilty using the term *normal*. If he
didn't reach a milestone at the expected time, was he then abnormal?
That was one word I couldn't even bear to say, as I substituted words
like *typical* or *typically-developing* as in, "He can't quite sit up like
a typical baby." In my heart I knew I was playing with semantics,
but I couldn't bring myself to think or say that anything about Caden
was abnormal.

That honest realization got me thinking about labels in a way
I never had before. As a teacher I had read and heard all about the
terms people use or don't use in an attempt for political correctness.
Was it better to say a person with disabilities rather than a disabled
person? Is using a phrase like *special needs* helpful or hurtful? Was

saying *normal* somehow disrespectful to others who didn't quite fit society's definition of that word?

"Let Caden be Caden," the Duke pediatrician's earlier words reverberated in my head as I tried to wrap my mind around these unsettling thoughts. Obviously every one of us is unique. We all have abilities and limitations, strengths and weaknesses, achievements and failures. I determined to try to let go of labels and instead rejoice in our beautiful, unique grandson. I wish I could say that I was completely successful. Being around other babies and toddlers, however, often evoked unexpected and overwhelming feelings of sadness. If I was alone with Caden, I could focus on his accomplishments and newly-developing skills. When I saw another eight-month-old, Caden's limitations were obvious and impossible to overlook. In my greatest moments of despair, my own mother's words echoed in my mind: *Stay strong and be positive. Go ahead and feel bad, but then pull yourself together.* I gained much strength and comfort from my memories of her.

Now when Laurie put Caden through his exercises, I was amazed at the progress he'd made since I had last seen him. Laurie had been having Caden work out with a fitness ball to gain neck strength. Initially he had hated "tummy time" on the floor because he had trouble lifting his head without doing a nosedive. Finally he was able to lie face down on the ball and raise his head. Another milestone to celebrate. Although some babies could have picked up their heads like this shortly after birth, we were just happy that Caden had accomplished it at all.

I was reminded of a quote by Joan Ryan, author of *The Water Giver: The Story of a Mother, a Son, and Their Second Chance.* I had begun using it as a tagline in my emails: "Motherhood is about raising and celebrating the child you have, not the child you thought you would have. It's about understanding that he is exactly the person he is supposed to be. And that, if you're lucky, he just might be the teacher who turns you into the person you are supposed to be."

Slowly and imperfectly we were learning how to be the kind of parents and grandparents that Caden needed.

One afternoon Laurie and I took Caden to a nearby park. He loved riding through the neighborhood in his stroller and looking at the pretty fall colors on the trees overhead. Walking down the street in the warm sunshine, I cherished the experience of pushing my grandson to the playground. How bad could Caden's condition be, I thought, if I could still take my grandson on an outing like any other grandmother?

Lifting him out of the stroller, we carefully placed him in the infant swing with the bucket seat. Slowly we pushed him back and forth, hoping he would be able to hold his head steady in spite of his weak neck muscles. Although we barely pushed him a couple of inches in either direction, Caden loved the experience of moving forward and back. For a perfect moment, we were any mom and any gramma taking our baby to the playground on a beautiful fall afternoon.

One morning later in the week, while Laurie was busy upstairs, I walked out on the front porch with Caden to get some fresh air. Although Caden only weighed a little over fifteen pounds, he always felt like dead weight because of his poor muscle tone. His body lacked that typical rigidity of most infants. Even newborns have a certain amount of tension in their bodies, but Caden always felt limp in my arms. Picking him up was like lifting a sleeping child. Sometimes I joked that we needed to start feeding him some starch. As I cradled him upright in my left arm that day, I noticed how much more steadily he was now able to hold his own head upright. Although he was definitely getting stronger, I rested my right hand firmly against his back, just in case.

For a while we just stood looking at the colored leaves on the trees in the front yard. The next-door neighbor Scott gave us a friendly wave as he worked on some outside chores. The sun felt warm on my face, and I noticed the softness of Caden's hair brushing my cheek as I kissed him on the top of his head. That sweet smell of a baby's head brought a smile to my lips as I cuddled him close in my arms.

In the midst of my reverie, I noticed the emptied garbage can sitting at the bottom of the driveway. I'll just walk out to the street and retrieve it, I thought. Then I can return it to its spot beside the garage. Strolling down the driveway, I carefully held on to Caden while I talked softly in his ear about what we were going to do. Dragging the large wheeled trash can with one hand back up the steep, sloping driveway, I was careful to keep Caden's body tightly against my side. My elbow rested under his bum, and my left hand, with fingers splayed widely, cradled his back. Stowing the trash can neatly beside the garage, I walked slowly and carefully toward the tall brick steps leading back up to the front porch.

Cautiously I took hold of the white wooden railing with my right hand and stepped up first with my left foot. Catching the toe of my flip-flop on the edge of the brick step, I swung violently to the right against the railing and sat down hard on my left hip with my left side and ribs cracking into the step above. Caden's head whipped back and forth as I instinctively tried to shelter him from the force of my fall, but I had no time to really spare him. The only thought that flashed through my mind was that his head was going to hit the brick step. He was going to get hurt.

Every bone in my body jarred painfully, but what I heard first were Caden's screams. Immediately I saw that his forehead had a nasty scratch above his right eye. Had his head actually hit the step at full force? I had fallen so hard. He seemed mostly just scared, but I couldn't be sure. In shock and terror, I struggled to my feet and limped the rest of the way up the stairs. Yelling for Laurie, I pushed open the front door. Looking up, I saw Laurie practically flying down the steps from the second floor bedroom. As Caden's screams echoed through the house, a look of pure panic flooded her face. Tears immediately filled her eyes.

"Mom, what happened?"

"I fell coming up the front steps with him." My voice caught in my throat, and I could barely say the words.

Laurie grabbed Caden from my arms, hugging and shushing him as she checked him over. He had the obvious scrape on his forehead, and her further examination revealed a small cut on the top of his head and a tiny bump under his chin. Fairly quickly Caden calmed down, and his screams turned to the occasional whimper. Surely, I prayed, if his head had really banged forcefully against the step, as I had first thought, he would look much worse. Still, we were not about to take any chances.

Laurie carried Caden out to the car while I scrambled around grabbing the diaper bag, Laurie's purse, and the car keys. After buckling him into his car seat, Laurie crawled into the back beside him while I jumped behind the wheel. Quickly turning the key in the ignition, I took a few deep breaths to calm myself. No longer even aware of the beautiful fall day, I carefully backed out into the street and headed for the nearest ER while Laurie gave directions as I drove.

Guilt ridden, my hands shook so badly I could hardly drive. Glancing into the rear-view mirror, I could see the calm but concerned look on Laurie's face.

"How's he doing?" I asked, hearing the fear in my own voice.

Caden was no longer crying.

"He's doing okay, Mom."

Laurie had assured me that the ER wasn't far, but as I drove the unfamiliar streets, the trip seemed to be taking forever. The accident kept replaying in my head like a nightmare. Why had I worn those stupid flip-flops? Why had I gone off the porch to get the trash can? Even as I had walked out to the street to retrieve it, I had briefly wondered if holding Caden with just one arm would be safe on my return trip up the driveway while pulling the can. But it had seemed like such a simple task. Just trying to be helpful. Why hadn't I listened to my instincts? How could I have been so careless?

After about twenty of the longest minutes I have ever endured, we finally arrived at the ER. I stopped at the entrance to let Laurie and Caden out before parking the car in the nearby lot. Entering the waiting room, I quickly sat down and held Caden so Laurie could check in at the desk. Resting comfortably in my lap, he seemed perfectly fine except for the telltale scrape on his forehead, which thankfully wasn't even bleeding.

As I looked around the room, I saw lots of chairs filled with other patients. One man was in a wheelchair. Another family sat across from me with a preschooler and an infant. From their conversation I inferred that the baby had a cold and the ER was their doctor's office of choice. Various other people wandered in and out. Soon Laurie came over and sat down beside us. We would have to wait our turn.

After what seemed like an eternity, the nurse called Caden's name, and he and Laurie disappeared through some doors on their way back to an examination room. Sitting alone while waiting, I felt time passing slowly. Fretfully I twisted my fingers and realized that I was actually wringing my hands. My foot bounced nervously as I crossed my legs.

After a few minutes, the receptionist looked up from her paperwork. "Would you like to go back with your daughter and grandson?"

"May I?"

"Of course," she answered kindly.

Directed back to the examination room through a maze of corridors and swinging doors, I eventually found Caden sitting calmly in his diaper on the exam table while the ER doctor checked him over carefully from head to toe.

"I'm the grandmother," I explained as I walked into the room. You know, the stupid one who fell with her grandson, I thought.

Laurie's composed expression was reassuring. The doctor continued his exam. His comments were punctuated with repetitive nods and a-hums, utterances that felt oddly comforting.

"Everything seems to be okay," he remarked. "You have two choices. We can keep him here for a few hours under observation; and if all goes well, you can go home. Or, we can do a CAT scan of his head to totally rule out any bleeding or injury. Unfortunately, a CAT scan at this young age is not without risks. It could increase his lifetime chances of developing a brain tumor."

Oh, great, I thought. Not only have I caused all of today's trauma, but I could now be responsible for him someday developing brain cancer.

"Let me call my husband," said Laurie.

After a quick phone conversation, they opted for observation; and I breathed a small sigh of relief. Zach was actually driving home from his conference at the time and was only a few miles away. He would arrive shortly.

The doctor left us alone in the room with a few simple instructions of what to watch for in Caden's behavior. Laurie began to redress a now calm and happy boy.

"Mom, I have to warn you. Zach may be pretty upset over this."

"I know. I'm so sorry."

I could only imagine how Laurie and Zach must both be feeling. Zach and I had developed a closeness since Caden's birth, nurtured by our shared love and concern for this precious child. That my misstep might irrevocably damage that bond broke my heart.

As Laurie sat down with Caden on her lap, I paced nervously. The tiny room held the usual exam table and medical equipment with little space for even the two of us. The blank walls and cold tile floor provided no comfort or distraction. Why oh why did this have to happen? I felt miserable. What if Zach couldn't forgive me? What if he didn't trust me around Caden anymore? Looking over at Caden playing quietly in Laurie's arms, I felt somewhat confident that he was going to be all right. The scrape above his right eye looked like a skinned knee. He also had a red mark under his chin and a tiny cut hiding under his hair. Surely if he were badly hurt, the visible damage would be worse. Perhaps what I saw out of the corner of my eye as I fell was more his head flailing back and forth than any forceful contact. Perhaps I had taken the brunt of the fall after all. Please, God, let him be fine, I prayed.

In a matter of minutes, Zach arrived. He had rushed straight to the hospital as soon as he had gotten back into town. Zach is always calm and controlled, but I could see the look of apprehension on his face as he entered the cubicle. Quickly he approached Caden. His eyes scanned Caden from top to bottom while assessing his injuries.

"Oh, that doesn't look so bad," he murmured.

"Oh, Zach, I'm so, so sorry," I said. "I never meant to hurt him."

"It's okay, Mom. I was expecting much worse. He looks fine. I know it was an accident. I just hope you won't be afraid to take care of him now."

"I was afraid you wouldn't trust me with him again."

"Are you kidding? It was just an accident."

My eyes flooded with tears of relief. Suddenly the future looked less bleak.

"We need to run home and get Caden's formula," said Laurie. "He needs to eat, and the hospital doesn't have the special formula he takes. And Zach needs to return the state car to the lab and pick up our other car. Would you be comfortable staying here with Caden?"

Gently she placed him in my arms. The doctor had approved allowing Caden to fall asleep, and already his eyes were looking drowsy. I cuddled him close, and his eyes shut before Laurie and Zach left the room. Looking down at our sweet boy, I silently thanked God for keeping him safe. How could I bear anything else bad happening to this child? He already had so much to handle; he didn't deserve more discomfort. Again it seemed that God had shielded him. A close call with serious injury had been averted. Laurie and Zach had just now confidently left him in my care. That they still trusted me was a gift I cherished. Tears filled my eyes again as I held Caden a bit tighter while he peacefully slept.

Within the hour Laurie and Zach returned. By the time they had Caden fed, the doctor was ready to discharge him.

"Just keep a close eye on him for the next two days. Wake him every few hours during the night just enough to see that he stirs. I think he's going to be just fine."

Gratefully, we gathered our things and headed home.

The final few days of my visit, I was subjected to a lot of gentle teasing. Facebook posts and photos of Caden's forehead circulated among friends. Everyone who heard our story seemed to have his or her own tale to tell. Hardly a baby alive, it seemed, had avoided being dropped. Rolling off a piece of furniture or getting pinched fingers appeared to be an infant's rite of passage. Even my own sister reminded me of how our mother had let her roll off the top of the washing machine where she had laid her to change her diaper. None of these accounts fully eased my guilt, but I suspected that this incident would also eventually become a family story to be told and retold over Thanksgiving dinners or birthday celebrations. Remember when Gramma tripped up the steps while carrying Caden, and he hit his head and had to go to the emergency room? I would easily endure that story now that I knew it had a happy ending.

When we got home from the hospital, I threw my flip-flops into the trash. I couldn't bear to ever look at them again.

Once more the time arrived too quickly for my return to Maine. Leaving never seemed to get any easier. At least most babies heal quickly, and Caden was no different. His scrapes were fading fast, and he was having no ill effects from our accident. Arriving at the airport, I consoled myself with our holiday plans. Laurie, Zach, and Caden would be flying to our house in Maine for Christmas. Our whole family would be together for the first time in eighteen months. I had that to look forward to, and Christmas would arrive before I knew it. With that thought for comfort, I got on the plane and headed home.

Chapter 20

"God is our refuge and strength,
an ever present help in trouble."
Psalm 46:1

Another month passed, and Caden continued to make progress. On November fourteenth he celebrated his nine-month birthday by waking up with his first TWO teeth! That event, rather than the recent time change, seemed to account for his crankiness and sleeping difficulties during the previous week.

Our little guy was now doing a really great job of sitting up by himself. When they had seen the pediatric neurologist at Duke in October, he had asked, "Now he can't sit up yet, can he?"

Laurie and Zach quickly responded, "Oh, yes, he can!"

Caden was happy to demonstrate, and the doctor was delighted.

Turning to the entourage of students standing behind him, he said, "If you had seen this baby when he was first born, you wouldn't believe he can do this today."

Almost a month later, Caden could not only sit, but he could also happily play with his toys while doing so. Only when a toy rolled out of reach, or he threw it too far, did trouble ensue. Bending over as far as he could, stretching and reaching without success, he would wail in frustration. He so much wanted to crawl, but his arms just weren't strong enough yet, and his weak neck muscles were still unable to hold up his heavy head. Not to be deterred, however, he succeeded in rolling over and back or over and over all the way across the floor to get what he wanted. Laurie discovered the latter accomplishment when she went into the kitchen one morning to get his formula and returned to the living room to find Caden chewing on one of the dog's toys.

Even more encouraging, Caden could now support his own weight on his legs for brief spurts, so he could stand steadily for a few seconds at a time. He couldn't pull himself up to a standing position yet, but he could hang on to the edge of the couch if someone put him there.

Feeding, as always, remained a stumbling block. The doctors wanted his formula increased by five milliliters per feed per week. Trying that just caused him to throw up even more. As Laurie lamented, "Five milliliters is a ridiculously small amount to affect him like that."

I tried reminding her of the times when I left a single bite of food on my plate. That too seemed silly. Perhaps Caden was experiencing a baby version of "when I'm full, I'm full." At least he had started doing some sign language for food including the sign for *milk*. Laurie determined to teach him *all done*. At least then, she thought wistfully, he might let her know before he threw up.

Later in November, Caden was scheduled for urological surgery at Duke. At the time of his birth, the pediatric urologist who was going to circumcise him noticed that he had a slight malformation of the external opening of the urethra, a fairly common condition seen in baby boys. Since this required a bit more repair than the doctor wanted to perform on a sick newborn, the procedure was postponed. Now the time had arrived to remedy this problem.

As the urologist told Laurie and Zach, "You don't want him peeing on his shoes when you start to toilet train him."

Once again, surgery meant another anesthetic and the accompanying risks. Maybe they should just skip the circumcision for now, I thought, since the circumcision wasn't absolutely necessary. But then again, the urological repair was, and both could be taken care of at the same time. The anesthesiologist decided to use the same anesthesia he had used during the insertion of Caden's feeding tube months earlier. All we could do was sit and wait and pray for good results.

This time Jay and I were at home in Maine, and Laurie and Zach were at the hospital with Caden by themselves. Waiting for the phone to ring with updates from Laurie proved even more difficult than actually being at the hospital ourselves. Time passed slowly as we tried busying ourselves around the house with mindless chores. Not wanting to stray too far from the phone, we paced the house like two trapped animals.

During the surgery, two different specialists took turns checking out and repairing Caden's medical issues. First, the gastroenterologist did an endoscopy to view everything from Caden's esophagus to his small intestine. He took tissue samples and looked for any possible cause of Caden's frequent vomiting. He wanted to make sure there was no apparent physical reason for Caden's feeding issues. Fortunately, all looked normal.

The urologist then determined that on closer inspection, Caden's urinary abnormality was insignificant and actually required no repair. However, she discovered that Caden had a small hernia that needed some attention. She proceeded to fix that problem successfully. Finally, Caden was circumcised and then wheeled off to the recovery room. Both the surgery and the anesthetic had gone well, and in a few weeks the doctor would follow up with an ultrasound to make sure everything had healed properly. After a pretty uncomfortable night, Caden was discharged the next day.

The next two weeks passed without any complications as Caden healed. He was pretty sore, especially the first few days, but slowly he began to return to his usual happy self. The gastroenterologist called to say that all the biopsies from Caden's endoscopy had come back normal. There were still no definitive answers for Caden's sensitive tummy, just the continuing hope that the issue would resolve itself as Caden grew older and stronger. Easy for a doctor to say, but not so easy to live with day in and day out. All in all, however, the trip to surgery had been successful, and another necessary medical intervention could be checked off the list.

One day after Caden was well enough to resume outings away from home, Laurie took him to the local supermarket. Caden loved riding through the store in the cart while looking around at all the activity and other people. As he and Laurie made their way up and down the aisles, he smiled and babbled happily at the other customers. Finished with her shopping, Laurie got in the line for a cashier. While standing there patiently awaiting their turn, suddenly without warning, Caden threw up all over the floor. The horrified guy in line behind them quickly backed up.

"Welcome to my world," Laurie sighed.

A simple trip to the grocery with Caden was never really simple, just life as they knew it. How grateful we would all be when Caden was able to eat normally and keep the food down. Some days we had trouble believing that time would ever come.

Chapter 21

"Answer me when I call to you, O my righteous God.
Give me relief from my distress;
be merciful to me and hear my prayer."
Psalm 4:1

In early December, Caden returned to Duke to see the pediatric pulmonologist again. Usually Laurie and Zach made these trips together, but on that particular day Zach was called to testify in court on a case he was investigating. As a forensic biologist for the North Carolina State Crime Lab, he primarily worked with DNA evidence, and sometimes he was required to explain his findings during a trial. On that particular day, the case was being tried in Durham, where Duke is located. Laurie drove to Duke alone with Caden, and the day had gotten off to a stressful start. Luckily Zach's testimony finished quickly, and he met Laurie and Caden at the doctor's office by the time of the appointment.

At this visit Caden had to repeat the pulmonary function tests, which the pulmonologist had first administered when he was six months old. CFTD primarily affects the skeletal muscles, which control gross motor skills. To some extent, however, the muscles that help a person breathe, cough, etc. can also be weaker. Caden's tests that day would show how much that muscle weakness was affecting him. The tests are very uncomfortable for the patient and very difficult to perform accurately on a child, especially one as young as ten-month-old Caden. Laurie and Zach hated to have to put him through it again, but the doctors insisted that closely monitoring his lung function was necessary. Once more Caden was hooked up to equipment that made him feel like he was trying to breathe through a straw. Watching him struggle was heartrending for Laurie and Zach. The results, however, were encouraging. His lung function, while not normal, had improved a bit since his checkup four months earlier. The doctor deemed him "not normal but not too abnormal."

This was great news since it meant no respiratory therapy or mechanical intervention was yet required. The pulmonologist, however, recommended that Caden receive a series of Synagis shots during the winter months to prevent him from contracting the serious respiratory infection known as RSV. The series is expensive, thousands of dollars, and not usually approved by insurance for an older baby. After receiving letters from the pulmonologist and pediatrician, the insurance finally agreed to pay. Another prayer answered.

Since Caden's birth, the medical bills continued to mount, and Laurie and Zach were inundated with the paperwork required to keep all the medical records sorted. Although Caden was covered by the State Employees Insurance of North Carolina through Zach's workplace, the co-pays and deductibles alone stretched their finances to the breaking point.

Family and friends continued to help as they were able, but Laurie and Zach further postponed some recommended therapies because they just didn't have the money to pay for them. Laurie was trying to work some evenings and Saturdays, scheduling her appointments when Zach could be home with Caden, but any income from her work as a massage therapist was unpredictable and intermittent at best. Zach began to talk about trying to find a job overseas.

"With my science background, I could get a job abroad with a private contractor. In four to six months, I could earn enough money to put a dent in our expenses."

"How would I manage with Caden and without Zach for months?" Laurie cried when I talked to her on the phone. "He's really serious about this, Mom, and has been in contact with a recruiter."

I tried to comfort and reassure her, but inside I was scared to death he might really try to do this. Zach's commitment to his family on every level was unshakeable, and I knew he would do everything humanly possible to take care of Laurie and Caden. The enormity of even considering such a decision showed his love for them and the desperation he felt. Fervently I prayed it wouldn't come to that.

Luckily, before Zach could pursue working abroad any further, they received their final approval for the CAP-C program through the Katie Beckett Waiver that gave them access to Medicaid funding for Caden. They had been waiting six months for Caden to qualify and then to reach the top of the waiting list. This would not solve all their financial challenges, but Zach was able to quit thinking about working abroad.

At last Caden was able to restart his professional physical therapy. A therapist named Chip replaced Nancy, and he was very pleased with Caden's progress. He was also kind enough to credit Caden's advances to all the time and effort Laurie and Zach had put into working with him on their own. At Chip's initial evaluation, Caden's fine motor skills were deemed age appropriate; and his gross motor skills were showing marked improvement.

By December Caden was sitting up really well. He could also now hold his own weight and balance himself briefly when someone stood him on his feet. He had not, however, mastered crawling, and Chip did not want him skipping this important developmental step.

Chip arrived one morning with a very strange contraption to help Caden learn to crawl.

"Let's see if this helps," he said.

He got Caden situated so that he was lying on his tummy in a crawling position with a sling-like piece of the equipment holding up his belly. The contraption moved on wheels, and when properly used, would allow Caden to get the sensation of crawling while also strengthening his limbs. The first time Chip placed him in the apparatus, Caden immediately screamed, gagged, and threw up.

"Mom, I just wanted to yell at Chip to stop. I knew what was coming, but he just kept pushing Caden," complained Laurie when she called me later.

"I know. That must be awful to watch, but you just have to believe Chip knows what he's doing."

Still my heart hurt for her. Seeing your own child's discomfort is miserable, and Laurie had seen it way too many times.

Caden continued to maneuver successfully by rolling, but it was obvious that his inability to crawl was becoming very frustrating for him. In between weekly physical therapy visits, Laurie continued to work with him on her own, and slowly Caden began to scream less and cooperate more.

In spite of his physical challenges, Caden remained a very happy baby. He clapped his hands, smiled and laughed easily, and loved the company of other people. He enjoyed playing with his toys, and bath time was the highlight of his day. His head control and balance steadily improved, and he was soon able to sit and even bounce a bit on his new riding toy, our early Christmas gift.

Laurie continued her search for a speech/feeding therapist. A few had turned them down as clients because they didn't feel qualified to work with a baby with Caden's particular diagnosis. No one had ever even heard of CFTD.

As for talking, Caden did say *Da-Da* and was working on *Ma-Ma*. He babbled away while he played and showed all the right signs of developing language, but his attempts at oral feeding were still pretty unsuccessful. When Caden was given the G-tube at five weeks, the doctors had felt that he would only need it temporarily, perhaps for a few weeks or months until he did better with the bottle. Here it was almost ten months later, and he was no longer taking any bottle at all. That plus the constant vomiting, especially when they tried to increase his feeds, was proving very frustrating and discouraging.

"Mom, it's so hard sometimes to hear other mothers complain that their babies have this little issue or that little problem. I just want to scream, 'I feed my baby through a tube!'"

"I know. And I'm sure there are mothers whose children are even more severely affected who feel that way when you complain about feeding, and they wish theirs could just sit up."

"You're right, of course, but it is still so hard."

And it's hard being your momma, I thought, never knowing what the right thing was to say. Should I be sympathetic? Should I be realistic? Should I just keep my mouth shut? What would help her the most? What was right? Often, I just didn't know.

This journey we were on had lots of questions but very few answers. We just had to trust we were doing the best we could and hope that was enough.

Chapter 22

"For God so loved the world that He gave His one and only Son,
that whoever believes in Him shall not perish
but have eternal life."
John 3:16

As December progressed and the holidays drew closer, we looked forward to Laurie, Zach, and Caden's visit. This would be Caden's first plane ride and the first time in a couple of years that our whole immediate family would be together for Christmas. I passed the days until their arrival trying to make everything perfect. I carefully decorated the house and tree, searched for just the right gifts, and baked everyone's favorite treats. We had so much to be joyful about this year. Nothing was going to diminish my thankfulness.

One Sunday during Advent, our pastor in Maine preached a sermon on the Virgin Mary. He said that Mary waited with courage, hope, and the promise that she was part of God's plan and a blessing to the world. I too felt like I was just waiting. As patiently as I could, I waited with courage, aided by the concerns and prayers of family and friends. I waited with hope, sustained by my faith. And I waited with the certain knowledge that Caden was truly a blessing from a God who had a very special plan for this baby. Hearing the minister's words and feeling God's presence at that moment brought me immense comfort. How amazing that whenever my faith and trust wavered, something unexpected would happen to reassure me of God's presence and peace.

The Saturday before Christmas finally arrived. Zach, Laurie, and Caden flew into Logan Airport in Boston where my other son-in-law Rick picked them up and drove them to Maine. Caden's first airplane ride went better than expected. Despite some passengers' negative opinions of the TSA employees, they seemed to have a soft spot for a mom, dad, and baby weighed down with all kinds of potentially suspicious material: liquid medicine, special formula, and medical equipment including a feeding pump. They kindly ushered our family through security, and Caden rewarded them all with smiles and perfect travel manners.

I could hardly wait for everyone to arrive at the house. Several months had passed since I had last seen Caden, and I could barely contain my excitement. Sometimes I feared our adult children must feel a bit snubbed when I rushed right past them to scoop up a grandbaby out of their arms. I'm not sure if they were all being good-natured and forgiving or if they were just grateful to have an extra pair of helping hands offered so willingly.

I was amazed by all the progress Caden had made since my last visit in early October. He had definitely added more babbling and new consonants to his vocabulary. I heard for myself the occasional Ma-Ma and Da-Da. He had also learned to clap his hands, and he was now sitting steadily.

One afternoon I decided to teach him how to hold his arms up in the air and play "So Big."

"How big is Caden?" I cooed. "So big!" I exclaimed while taking his hands and raising them over his head.

In less than a minute, he was throwing his arms up in the air by himself in response to every one of my "how bigs." A huge grin spread across his face as he responded to my cheers of approval. A tiny bit of tenseness inside me relaxed, again reassured by this simple bit of "normal" baby behavior.

132

By then Caden was trying hard to pivot and crawl from a sitting position. He was able to get one leg over, but he couldn't quite yet support his own weight on his arms enough to get up on his knees. Not easily discouraged, he just rolled to whatever he wanted. A favorite spot was under the Christmas tree with the beautiful lights and dangling ornaments. I had kept the lower branches free of any breakables, but he loved to lie there and either bat away at the soft ornaments within his reach or just stare in awe at the twinkling lights. Watching him reminded me of our own two girls as babies doing the very same thing. Every familiar gesture served to reassure me that in so many ways, Caden's development was just like any other baby's. He was doing much better than anyone had at first expected, and I was so grateful.

Although we rejoiced in his achievements, at ten months Caden could still not get himself from lying down to sitting up. Neither could he crawl across the room nor pull himself up to standing from sitting. When we held him upright by his hands, however, he immediately tried to move his own feet across the floor. For months we had hoped his legs and core would get strong enough to support his weight. Now that he could stand, we began to think that someday he would be able to walk. Such a determined little guy he was proving to be.

Our four-year-old granddaughter Cate loved meeting her baby cousin for the first time. She played the role of little mother beautifully as she kept Caden entertained with his toys. Over and over he put blocks into containers and took them out. He banged objects together or hammered one with the other. Thankfully, he was showing no difficulty using his hands.

Caden also thoroughly enjoyed playing with Cate's little Fischer Price drum set, the very toy his aunt and mommy played with as babies. After bringing it out of storage after all those years, I delighted in watching the next generation enjoying it too. Actually I had a whole cupboard filled with a barn, doll house, village, toy airplane and lots of plastic people that had been stored away years before in the attic in our house in Ohio. When we moved to Maine in 2009, I insisted on bringing those toys along. I'm sure Jay inwardly thought this was a crazy idea, but he humored me. Now in our living room, with the lights shimmering on the Christmas tree and a fire in the fireplace, our grandchildren sat playing contentedly. I smiled as all seemed very right in my world.

On Christmas Eve I was looking forward to the whole family worshiping together at the Episcopal church we attended in Maine. Because of Caden's schedule, the timing of the service wasn't particularly convenient. I knew the 9:00 PM service would be well past his bedtime. The children's service was scheduled for 4:00 PM. That was a perfect time for most little ones, after naps and before dinner. Caden wasn't most children, however, and that was the exact time he had his third bolus feed of the day.

"Mom, do you think the service will be very long?" Laurie asked. "If not, we'll just feed him a bit late."

Considering this was Christmas Eve, I guessed the Episcopalians would never cut things short, even for the kids. I was also afraid if I admitted to that, Laurie and Zach would decide not to go to church with us. I so wanted to show off Caden to all my fellow friends and parishioners who had so regularly and faithfully prayed for this baby they had never even seen. So, feeling guilty even as the words popped out of my mouth, I lied.

"I don't think it will be too long."

We all got dressed for church, and Caden looked adorable in his Christmas outfit. He had dark green corduroy pants, a white turtleneck, and a sweater with a moose on the front, the perfect Maine Christmas attire.

We arrived at a church packed with familiar faces. Fragrant pine wreathes and colorful poinsettias created a warm, welcoming scene. Candles flickered magically, and Christmas carols played softly in the background. As I settled into the pew next to Jay, I looked down the row beside me at our two daughters, sons-in-law, and Cate and Caden all gathered together. My heart swelled with joy. What a blessing that we could all be together on this special night.

As the service wore on, I began to feel increasingly anxious. Laurie glanced my way with raised eyebrows, her unspoken question plainly reflected in her facial expression: When is this going to be over?

"Soon," I mouthed.

No Episcopal service will be complete without communion, I thought to myself, as the service slowly continued. Would it never end? Luckily, Caden was being the perfect child. There were definitely some advantages to the fact that he never seemed to get hungry on his own or at least recognize the feeling enough to complain.

At last the final prayer was said, and the service ended. Lots of friends crowded around us as we made our way toward the doors. They were anxious to welcome Caden and see this child for whom they had prayed so fervently. My heart swelled with thankfulness and pride as I absorbed their attention to my family.

Luckily, Laurie and Zach forgave me for my deception about the length of the service.

"We would STILL have gone, Mom. We just would have taken formula with us and found a quiet place to feed him when the service ran late."

"Oh," I said sheepishly.

No grandmother of the year award for me. Fortunately, Caden wasn't fazed by his delayed dinner. Little did he know that his late meal had given his gramma her best Christmas gift ever, all the family together at church for Christmas Eve.

We opened our presents on Christmas morning. While we sent most of the kids' gifts to North Carolina early so they wouldn't have to deal with getting packages home on the plane, we had stockings to open, a few extra small toys for Caden, and the traditional family coffee cake to eat. Lindsay, Rick, and Cate joined us after they had opened Santa's gifts at their home, and all eight of us enjoyed the day together, sharing food, fun, and family time.

I loved watching Cate hover over her younger cousin, gently entertaining him with toys and her attention. Those sweet hugs she gave him melted my heart. As we sat gathered around the fireplace, I couldn't help but think of all we had been through in the past year. With the many fears and worries over Caden's health issues momentarily in the background, just enjoying this Christmas together as a family was a treasure I would long remember. I felt wrapped in a blanket of love and peace.

What would Christmas in Maine be like without a snowfall? In preparation I had gone to the local consignment shop and bought Caden an adorable snowsuit for his visit. The morning we all awoke to flakes covering the ground and continuing to fall, Laurie and Zach decided to introduce Caden to his first sled ride.

Dressed in his snowsuit, Caden looked like a little tan furry lion replete with a hood decorated with ears and a mane. Laurie set him on a sled she had ridden on herself as a child. Then she sat down behind him and pulled him snugly between her legs. Zach grabbed the rope and off they all went down the snow-covered private road in front of our house.

Caden's eyes widened with surprise as he bounced along. The snowsuit was a bit too big on him, and he reminded me of Randy from the movie *Christmas Story,* with his arms stuck out to the side and his tiny face peeking out from inside the furry hood. I had to laugh, but I loved seeing him enjoy another simple kid activity.

The rest of the visit passed way too quickly. Before I knew it, Laurie and Zach had packed their suitcases and were ready to return to North Carolina. Lindsay and I drove them to Logan Airport in Boston so they could get a direct flight to Raleigh. After I dropped them off at Departures and headed back north, the car felt way too quiet and empty. If only, I thought, they lived here in Maine near us. That, however, would probably not be the best for them. They needed to be close to the good medical care they received at Duke. Furthermore, they enjoyed living in the South. Laurie had never been a cold weather gal, and I knew she loved the North Carolina climate. If they were closer, Jay and I could be so much more help to them, but I knew I had to accept God's plan and trust in His will. Surely we were all exactly where we were meant to be at this particular time in our lives. I certainly hoped so because I was going to miss them terribly.

Chapter 23

"But I will sing of your strength,
in the morning I will sing of your love;
for you are my fortress, my refuge in times of trouble."
Psalm 59:16

In the following weeks back in Clayton, Caden had several more checkups at Duke. First, he saw the urologist and gastroenterologist for post-surgical checkups. Both gave him a clean bill of health. He had healed beautifully.

The gastro guy, as I began to call him, was leaving Duke for another children's hospital in the Midwest, but one of his partners would take over Caden's care and would see him again in six months for a regular checkup. Laurie and Zach had grown close to Caden's doctors and had put their trust and confidence in their expertise. Losing one and having to adjust to another's care was difficult. The bond between the doctor, patient, and family can become unusually strong, especially with a child who has special medical needs. This is the man or woman who finally gave a diagnosis, performed that difficult procedure, or saved a life. A special connection was unavoidable. Caden was lucky to have had so many wonderful doctors, and this particular one would be missed.

That visit was followed by a second trip to Duke for another Special Infant Care Clinic. The trip itself was never easy, as the drive had to be arranged around Caden's feeding schedule, which often required getting up early to beat the rush hour traffic and then feeding Caden through his tube once they arrived at the hospital. Later they might need to fill some time until the doctor was ready for them. Then there was always the concern that Caden would be fussy or throw up all over them and himself. Laurie prepared by taking along multiple changes of clothes for all of them. It seemed, more times than not, those extra clothes were needed.

As usual, despite all the prodding and poking, Caden remained quite cooperative with the doctors. This visit he had his hearing rechecked. NICU babies, we learned, are at a greater risk for having hearing problems due to their early exposure to noisy monitors, beepers, and the general commotion of the nursery. After a thorough exam, the audiologist said Caden passed with flying colors.

Then it was on to his first real developmental evaluation by a child psychologist. Caden showed normal development in his cognitive, social, and fine motor skills. That word *normal* again. His gross motor skills, as expected, were delayed. At eleven months, he scored at the seven to eight month level. The doctor was still very pleased with these results. She told Zach and Laurie that it was a testament to their efforts working with him daily that he had improved so much and done so well. Since typically-developing babies learn by crawling and exploring, something Caden couldn't do yet, Laurie and Zach had provided Caden with lots of other learning opportunities. For now he was well on his way to achieving his own personal potential. When Laurie relayed this information to me on the phone at the end of the day, I couldn't help being reminded of the pediatric neurologist's advice months ago, "Let Caden be Caden."

Also in January, after many months of further applications, paperwork, evaluations, and approvals, Caden qualified for additional professional help. Not only would a physical and speech/feeding therapist come to the house to work with Caden once a week, but a Certified Nursing Assistant (CNA) would also help Laurie for twenty hours a week. In addition to those hours, she could provide occasional respite care. This assistance would surely help Caden, and it was a godsend for Laurie. Because of Caden's frequent bouts of vomiting, he could never be left alone even for a moment. Now Laurie could get a shower, complete some household chores, or even make a short trip to the grocery store knowing that Caden was under the watchful eye of another trained adult.

Well, in an ideal world, that was how it was supposed to work. In reality, her CNA often showed up late for work, canceled at the last moment, or even fell asleep on the job. She was good to Caden but not the most reliable. Some help, however, was better than none; and as long as Laurie herself was nearby, she at least felt as if she had a mother's helper and an extra pair of hands.

As Zach said, "Unless we had a NICU nurse from Duke helping out, we wouldn't feel completely comfortable. And Caden doesn't qualify for that."

I could hardly believe that almost a whole year had passed since Caden's birth. No day had gone by that I hadn't thought about, worried over, or rejoiced in Caden's life. Initially those thoughts had consumed nearly every waking moment. Eventually I was able to concentrate on other parts of my life as well, but not a day went by that I didn't hold Caden in prayer. He always occupied an important corner of my mind.

Considering the initial prognosis, Caden's physical progress had really been remarkable. After months of waiting, his therapies now continued in earnest. His physical therapist was still focusing on getting him to crawl. At this point Caden was really more interested in trying to walk, but the therapist stressed again the importance of not skipping the crawling stage. As a result, Caden continued to spend some time each week practicing in his crawling apparatus while protesting loudly.

The speech therapist was working in earnest on getting Caden to eat orally. She offered various spoons, gum massagers, and other oral utensils to get him used to different textures. He was still refusing most baby food, and when he did take a bite, it was really no more than a nibble. She warned Laurie that getting Caden to eat orally would be a long, slow process, a situation frustrating for both Caden and Laurie. Eating seems like such a normal activity for any one-year-old, but not Caden, who had been entirely tube fed for months. Caden also had a pretty strong gag reflex and frequently choked back up anything Laurie had been able to get him to swallow. If his daily experience with food often included vomiting, we could hardly blame him for his dislike of eating. Furthermore, he never really got hungry because his tube feeding schedule remained very regimented, and he hadn't begun to associate eating with pleasure.

Despite the CNA's shortcomings, she continued to help out, and a play therapist was about to begin working with Caden bi-weekly. With the occasional visits from case managers and supervisors, Laurie and Zach's home seemed to have acquired a revolving door. Having people coming and going every day was challenging, and Laurie felt as if she were always entertaining guests. Most days the benefits outweighed the inconvenience; nevertheless, the lack of privacy and the sense of intrusiveness could be unsettling. Fitting all the scheduled visits around Caden's tube feedings every three hours and his two daily naps required some rigorous scheduling. Laurie longed to call her home and family and personal life her own again. Those days, however, seemed over.

What made it all worthwhile were Caden's improvements. Although his attempts to crawl were still unsuccessful, he could finally push himself up to his knees; and he had found a way to push himself up from lying to sitting. Caden didn't always do things in the traditional way, but he always managed to figure out a way to succeed eventually. That trait was going to serve him well in life.

Soon he began to cruise slowly along the furniture. His ability to move his legs and feet forward if someone held onto both his hands also improved. Because his core strength was still weak, he tired easily and wobbled quite a bit. Sometimes while trying to walk, he would just put his head down on the couch or ottoman to rest a bit. He was definitely growing stronger day by day, but we parents and grandparents always found it hard to be patient. We rejoiced at every accomplishment, and then quickly searched for another sign of progress. We celebrated his successes, but the worries about his ultimate abilities continued to nag us. "Let Caden be Caden," continued to be our mantra and our comfort.

Despite his limitations, Caden loved to play with his toys. Much to his delight, the play therapist brought a box of new toys each time she visited, and Caden quickly developed his favorites. He especially liked the toys that made noise or had pieces that popped up. While sitting in his feeding chair for fifteen to twenty minutes four times a day, Caden often grew restless. Laurie tried to keep him interested in rattles, small books, and anything he could hold while sitting quietly. Sometimes she resorted to having Caden watch a DVD that taught sign language. He was fascinated and was quickly beginning to use a variety of signs himself: *milk, all done, dog, sleep*. As time passed, the list got longer and longer. He was learning so quickly, and we were all proud and grateful.

Chapter 24

"Be joyful always; pray continually;
give thanks in all circumstances,
for this is God's will for you in Christ Jesus."
1Thessalonians 5:16-17

Caden celebrated his first birthday in February. A few days before the big day, I flew to North Carolina to be there for his party. Unfortunately, Jay had to remain behind in Maine due to his work schedule. As his birthday approached, Laurie's happy excitement turned to melancholy.

"What's the matter, Laurie?" I asked, noting her gloomy mood.

"I just always thought of my baby eating his birthday cake and getting ice cream all over his face. You know, like you always see in other people's kids' first birthday pictures. That's just not going to happen with Caden, and it makes me a little sad."

With all Caden's victories and accomplishments, he would still probably not dig into his cake like a typical one-year-old. The face smeared with icing in the first birthday pictures would probably not be part of Caden's baby book. I too longed to celebrate exactly like other "normal" families did. How guilty and ungrateful I felt for having those thoughts.

In spite of those disappointments, we forged ahead with our plans for his first birthday party like any parent or grandparent might. Laurie decided on a music theme, and we decorated accordingly. We hung colorful streamers from the ceiling fan to the corners of the living room where more dangled from the French doors and twisted across the fireplace mantel. Multicolored balloons, including some fancy metallic ones, were tied to the mailbox and hung here and there inside the house. Caden batted and grabbed at everything with delight. His high chair had a special plastic birthday covering for catching ice cream drips and crumbs. Laurie had ordered a special birthday T-shirt for Caden to wear. On the front was an appliqued cupcake with his name and the words *First Birthday* embroidered underneath. Perfectly dressed for the occasion, he looked adorable. Now we just prayed he wouldn't throw up before his party and ruin his outfit.

A small gathering of friends and neighbors arrived in the afternoon for a simple celebration of ice cream and cake. A friend and work colleague of Zach's made Caden a yummy chocolate cake with blue icing in the shape of a guitar. The guitar strings were made from red licorice, and colored gummy candies provided further embellishments. Zach's dad, who traditionally makes the family birthday cakes, had brought a delicious double layer chocolate confection all the way from Ohio. We were right in guessing that Caden probably wouldn't be very interested in eating. Even his own little personal cupcake didn't tempt him, though he did take one tiny lick of the icing. "Let Caden be Caden," we all tried to remember.

In lieu of presents, Laurie and Zach had asked for donations to the Duke University Hospital's Ronald McDonald House. Several guests, however, brought small gifts; and Caden ripped off the wrapping paper with delight. As the neighbor children dashed through the house laughing and giggling and the adults mingled in conversation, I noticed Caden sitting on the floor looking happy and content. What a miracle baby. What a special blessing that he was even able to celebrate his first birthday. Caden himself was definitely the real gift at the party.

A whole year had passed since our family began this journey of love and faith with Caden. So many friends and family members had joined us for the ride. Even strangers had followed our story with prayers and concerns as email updates about Caden's progress got forwarded all over the world. The written responses, phone calls, prayers, meals, and donations had all supported us in ways we could never have imagined and could never repay. We had been so blessed as a family to have all these wonderful people in our lives. By reaching out to us, they had been our angels, providing us with strength and encouragement when we had none of our own.

One day in a mall parking lot, Laurie thanked a stranger who had changed her car tire for her when she had a flat.

"You're my guardian angel," she said gratefully.

"Oh, they're all around you," he replied. From the mouth of a stranger rang such words of truth.

On the day of Caden's birthday, Laurie posted the following on her Facebook page:

> A year ago today I had the privilege of participating in one of God's miracles by giving birth to our sweet Caden. What a bittersweet day it was. The overwhelming joy of meeting our baby boy for the first time was quickly replaced with overwhelming fear and sadness. In the days following we weren't even sure we'd get the opportunity to celebrate this glorious day.
>
> This year has been filled with many ups and downs, victories and challenges. But God has blessed Zach and me with the greatest gift we could have ever imagined and a love that grows stronger every day. Happy Birthday, Caden Zachary. We are honored to be your parents.

Reading that post, I knew how right his daddy had been when he said, "Caden is the perfect child for us, and we are the perfect parents for him." Someday Caden would know this too.

Epilogue

More than seven years have passed since that day when Jay and I became grandparents to our precious Caden Zachary. Caden has come a long way in that time, but there have been some setbacks. The most serious occurred when he was eighteen months old and contracted pneumonia. He spent two weeks in the hospital, much of it in intensive care. For a while the doctors thought he might even need to be intubated. His very life seemed in question.

After a frantic phone call from Laurie in the middle of the night, I flew to North Carolina the next day. Caden looked tiny and vulnerable lying in that big hospital bed with all the machines beeping and the tubes going everywhere. I experienced a sudden flashback to his early days in the NICU. Fear washed over me. Initially, Caden was wary of my presence. Was I another person in the room who might poke or jab him? Before long though, I had gained his trust, and he was soon snuggled in my arms, tubes and leads carefully arranged, while I rocked him contentedly. Eventually the antibiotics, IVs, breathing treatments, and aggressive respiratory therapy, including the use of a special machine called a cough assist, saved his life. By the time he was discharged, however, he had lost weight and was very weak. At first he could barely walk. It took several weeks for him to fully recover. That was by far the biggest health scare since his birth, but our prayers were answered, and he survived.

Caden developed cognitively on schedule except for his speech. For the longest time, he only said a few words, but he quickly learned to sign. He got so good at it that Laurie said he was practically signing in complete sentences. Once he finally started talking at about age three, his verbal communication progressed rapidly. He continues to have speech therapy at school to help with a few lingering articulation issues, but his vocabulary is extensive, and he talks nonstop. Now we often laugh at ourselves when we remember how worried we were that he would never talk. Today that's certainly not a problem.

Right after his third birthday, Caden started preschool in a small class for children with various disabilities. He did so well that he was soon moved to a different class with a blend of typically-developing children and those with various special needs. His ability to learn is not affected by his CFTD, and in preschool he proved himself to be a very smart little guy.

Caden's physical therapy continues both at school and privately. Although he learned to walk when he was fourteen months old, much earlier than anyone expected, his gross motor skills were definitely delayed. Frequent falls have always been an issue, and he can't always catch himself before crashing to the floor. As he told me once after a minor injury, "Gramma, it just makes me stronger." With practice and persistence, he has learned to do his own kind of "running" and "climbing," even though he does it slowly and with great effort and difficulty. His form may not be perfect, but his determination is.

In spite of his physical limitations, Caden loves sports. Unfortunately, participation remains challenging. When he tried t-ball one season, the coach and the other kids were very patient and supportive. Hitting the ball was manageable, but running to the base or picking a ball up off the ground was just too hard and too tiring. Undeterred, Caden moved on to other activities. One time when Zach, who is a runner, was going to compete in a race, Caden wanted to run with his daddy. So Zach did the running while pushing Caden in the jogging stroller. They were a team, and Caden loved it. When Zach was training for a half triathlon, he was working out on his stationary bike in the garage. Caden wanted to "train" also, so Zach rigged up Caden's little bike, which he can only ride with training wheels on a flat surface, into a stationary bike.

Caden loves telling me about these "workouts." Another day Caden told his dad that he wanted to do circuit training just like him. Zach created a course by having Caden "run" about twenty-five yards to the fence in the backyard and back, go up the three-foot climbing section of his swing set, and finish going down the slide. Although it required tremendous effort, Caden repeated the circuit over and over again while quietly whispering to himself, "Caden Kallenbach never quits."

The one place Caden can physically keep up with his friends is in the pool. In fact, he surpasses most of them. Caden loves the water and has become an excellent swimmer. The buoyancy of the water gives him a freedom he doesn't have on land. Because he prefers to swim mostly underwater, his chest muscles get a great workout as he holds his breath. Fun and therapy at the same time.

When Caden was old enough for kindergarten, he entered a regular class. He has made so many friends, and the other kids have been very understanding of his limitations. It is not unusual to see one of his buddies carrying his backpack for him, helping him up if he falls, or taking time out on the playground to join him on the swings while the other kids run around.

Caden is now in second grade and doing well academically. He likes reading and writing, but he will quickly tell you that math is his favorite subject. He does seem to have an aptitude for it. When recently asked what he wanted to do when he grew up, he said he'd like to work with computer forensics. He also says he'd like a job with a pension.

Perhaps most gratifying has been watching Caden's personality develop. He has a wonderful sense of humor and constantly entertains us with his funny comments. I am often touched by the empathy that he shows. We were watching a nature documentary one night on TV. The program included a scene where a baby orangutan was orphaned when his mother died. Caden was nearly inconsolable. He cried so long that we had to change the channel. Sensitive and caring, he is a kind, loving child with a sweet and gentle soul.

Caden's greatest medical victory so far has been the removal of his feeding tube. Shortly after he turned seven, his gastroenterologist and neurologist agreed that he no longer needed it. About two years prior, when Caden was five, his oral eating really started to improve. For so long Laurie and Zach had counted Caden's calories, measured his intake, monitored his weight, and taught and encouraged him to eat. Babies who are tube fed do not experience hunger the way everyone else does. They don't get hunger cues, and they don't necessarily associate eating with pleasure or social interaction. Furthermore, for those with muscle issues like Caden, eating is a lot of work. Transitioning from tube feeding to oral eating can take months or years. It is a very slow process in the best of circumstances, and sometimes it never happens. Eventually for Caden it did.

Taking the actual tube out was easy, but five months later surgery was required to close the opening where it had been inserted. Caden got through the surgery with a minimum of discomfort. In a few days, he was back to his normal activity; and in a few weeks, the only reminder of his ordeal was a one-inch scar. In Caden's words, "Mr. Leaky Hole is gone!"

Since Caden's birth, a lot more scientific studies are being done on congenital myopathies (muscle diseases) like his. Some promising treatments are in the beginning stages of clinical trials, and ongoing research is drawing attention to these rare genetic disorders. In recent years a nonprofit organization, The RYR-1 Foundation, has been established "to help raise awareness, educate, provide support, and raise funds for research for RYR-1 muscle disease." (from the RYR-1 Facebook page) At this time there is no treatment or cure, but there is hope.

As Caden's gramma, I am so proud of all that Caden has accomplished. Yes, if I'm honest, I'll admit to feeling a little sad sometimes when I realize some of his physical limitations because I know that life will be a bit harder for him. Sometimes those limitations make Caden sad too. More than anything he wishes he could run fast. In fact, when I recently told him that scientists were working on a treatment that might help his "special muscles," he looked up at me and said, "Well, I hope they hurry up because I really want to run fast."

Although we still do not know all that the future holds for Caden, I have no doubt he will overcome any challenges. The one thing I do know for sure is, "Caden Kallenbach never quits."

God has a special plan for Caden's life, and I can't wait to see how it all unfolds. Caden is and always will be the perfect child for us. The journey continues.

Acknowledgements

Thank you to my husband Jay. Your love and support helped to make my dream of writing this book a reality.

Thank you to all my family, including my sisters Kathy Glasmire and Diane Park, who encouraged me to write this book in the first place and who provided helpful feedback and enthusiastic cheerleading when I was ready to give up.

Thank you to William Newkirk; Diane Paterson; Judy Jenkins; Judy Newman; Laurie Kallenbach; Lindsay Davis; and Darreby Ambler, who was also my accountability buddy. These friends and family members spent hours reading, listening to, and commenting on early drafts. They helped me to clarify, to tighten, to elaborate, and to make my story better. There aren't enough words to convey my appreciation to all of you.

Thank you to the Congenital Fiber Type Disproportion (CFTD) Facebook group. Your posts and comments, your stories of struggles and victories made me certain that my story needed telling. In many ways, my story is your story. Your friendship across the miles means the world to me.

Thank you to The Guppies, the Freeport Maine Writing Group, and Elizabeth Peavey's Memoir Workshop. These three writing groups gave helpful feedback at various times during my lengthy writing and revision period.

Thank you to my copy editors, JoAnn Shade, Cindy Young, and Laurie Kallenbach. You helped me polish and perfect my manuscript.

Thank you to those friends and acquaintances who gave me publishing suggestions and advice or kept me writing by means of casual conversation or simple questions like, "How is your book coming along?" You were more motivation than you realized.

Thank you to my niece Jill Leonard McAmis for designing the cover.

Thank you to JoAnn Shade for helping me to finally get my book published. Without your help, it would still just be resting in my computer.

Finally, thank you to my mother, who always nurtured my love of reading and writing. If she were still alive, she would be so proud.

About the Author

Linda Sprague Pappas attended Bowling Green State University and graduated from Ashland College, now Ashland University, in Ohio with an English major and a B.S. in Education. She is a wife, mother, devoted grandmother to Cate and Caden, and a former high school English teacher. She enjoys spending time with her family and friends, reading, walking, playing the dulcimer, and practicing yoga. A native Ohioan, she now lives and writes in Midcoast Maine. She can be contacted at pappaslinda0@gmail.com.

33312021R00097

Made in the USA
Middletown, DE
14 January 2019